Books are to be returned on or
the last date

Critical Thinking for Better Learning

To follow knowledge like a sinking star,
Beyond the utmost bound of human thought.

—Alfred, Lord Tennyson, "Ulysses"

Critical Thinking for Better Learning

New Insights from Cognitive Science

Carole Hamilton

ROWMAN & LITTLEFIELD
Lanham • Boulder • New York • London

Published by Rowman & Littlefield
A wholly owned subsidiary of The Rowman & Littlefield Publishing Group, Inc.
4501 Forbes Boulevard, Suite 200, Lanham, Maryland 20706
www.rowman.com

Unit A, Whitacre Mews, 26-34 Stannary Street, London SE11 4AB

British Library Cataloguing in Publication Information Available

Library of Congress Cataloging-in-Publication Data Is Available

ISBN 978-1-4758-2778-1 (cloth : alk. paper)
ISBN 978-1-4758-2779-8 (paperback : alk. paper)
ISBN 978-1-4758-2780-4 (electronic)

∞™ The paper used in this publication meets the minimum requirements of American National Standard for Information Sciences—Permanence of Paper for Printed Library Materials, ANSI/NISO Z39.48-1992.

Printed in the United States of America

Contents

Preface

When I was in graduate school, our professor assigned a group of us to determine the reasons for the rise of the novel in the eighteenth century and to write our results in the form of a dialogue. Great, we thought, we can just bone up on the topic and talk—this will be easy! So we quickly coalesced as a group and started reading. However, very soon, I felt a wave of competitiveness. Would my comments be as smart as my teammates' insights? I decided to read more, think more, push my interpretations as far as I could. My friends had clearly done the same thing, so one can hear a lot of enthusiasm in the tape of our first session. We met a few more times to amplify our thoughts and finalize our theory, and loved every minute.

We developed the theory that novels served to help a growing middle class gain sophistication so they could advance in their social and economic world. We explained how the novel rose out of picaresque tales, the Grand Tour, conduct handbooks, and the like as a kind of training device for the ambitious new middle-class men and women who wanted to learn how to conduct themselves in higher society. Today I remember more about the rise of the novel than I do about any of the other ideas I learned in graduate school. Why was this project so satisfying? How did our professor so efficiently tap into our energy and willingness to collaborate in critical thinking? In fact, our theory has relevance to the topic of this book because two philosophers of that era, John Locke and David Hume, saw the mind as a tabula rasa, a blank slate, upon which knowledge and wisdom could be etched empirically,

> "We are motivated by knowledge gaps but put off by knowledge chasms."
>
> —Hattie and Yates 2013, 6

through observing, sensing, and interacting with the world. Their incipient accounts of learning lead directly to our current understanding of how people learn, which is that it happens through observing, sensing, and interacting with the world.

I already knew that I learned best by figuring things out myself, so the research and analysis part of our assignment was attractive. As you will read in this book, thinking and analyzing are attractive to all of us, as long as they are neither too simplistic nor too difficult. In addition, my tendency to question and even resist new ideas, a trait shared by my teammates, resulted not in conflict but in productive and engaged debate that led us to synthesize ideas and develop a stronger theory together. The joy and fulfillment we found in that project is something I want my own students to experience as often as they can. And I'd like them to experience it sooner in their educational careers than I did.

I have been an English teacher for twenty years, teaching students in grades six through twelve, but mostly at the high school level. During that time, having so many kinds of learners, I became interested in how people learn, with the goal of tuning my lessons to what would work best. Before the appearance of the new principles of cognitive science that ground this book, I had already designed lessons that asked students to analyze situations and information and to develop a theory. For example, I had them sift through examples and nonexamples (of grammar concepts, spelling conventions, etc.) in order to develop and confirm a rule. I also asked them, "What, if anything, is wrong with / good about this thesis / topic sentence / paragraph structure?" With this kind of close analysis, they became more discerning. The common thread was putting the responsibility for understanding on the student rather than asking students simply to accept what I said was true. Students also learned more when they had to do some research and create something with it. The more they learned, the more they cared about their projects, and having different students working on different topics enriched the whole class and made each student more confident. Discovery is fun. And it is wonderful to see a young person act, perhaps for the first time publicly, as an expert on something. It's also wonderful to hear how much they recall of those experiences when they visit me years later. Rich projects promote retention. But why? How?

As I used more of these kinds of methods, I started researching to discover why they worked so well. I attended some Learning and the Brain conferences. Although many of the conferences did not deliver the goods, a couple of the presenters linked empirical evidence of how people learn to neuroscience in a way that was quite revealing.

One of the most compelling insights came from cognitive scientists who said that we think by analogy. We store information in schemas that include both theory and organized chunks of information. Just conveying information alone does not create those crucial schemas, and without a theory or analogy to hold it together, the information just free-floats in memory, or is forgotten. Now I understood why students need both information and reasoning. However, if it was going to stick in their minds, they had to develop the reasoning themselves and understand it thoroughly.

Around this time, one of the physics teachers at my school was implementing a new teaching approach called modeling instruction (not at all the same as modeling, where the teacher demonstrates how to do a problem, and not the Common Core usage that calls problem solving "modeling") and having great success with it—retention and understanding rates doubled for his students, and students retained the knowledge for years. I confirmed this when two visiting alums (then seniors in college majoring in political science) were able to draw the eight models of physics mechanics at my request and to explain each in clear, precise language. In modeling instruction, students grapple with physics concepts through experimentation and observation, diagramming what they think is happening and developing a theory about it, long before hearing any formulas. I implemented a modeling instruction method for essay structure and developing thesis ideas, and never had to repeat those lessons, as I had had to do in prior years. This method of learning taps right into the way our brains learn—through thoughtful consideration and discerning what happens, then speculating why it does. The learned information gets efficiently stored alongside students' theories, in memory schemas that stick in the brain and become part of the students' worldview.

If students are going to learn how to think like practitioners, not just memorize information, then they will also begin to master the threshold concepts of the discipline, the portals of understanding that transform their thinking process. For example, an economics student who learns about opportunity costs will now make more informed decisions. A physics student who truly understands force gains a new, corrected perspective on motion and velocity. Her worldview has changed.

As practitioners, we sometimes take threshold concepts for granted, assuming they are obvious. But to our young students, they are not. Even when we teach these bedrock concepts directly, our students tend to cling to their own misconceptions instead. What's difficult is that often the threshold concepts challenge our students' worldview and they respond by resisting them, oversimplifying them, learning them just for the test. Therefore, rather than moving from one discrete lesson unit to the next, we need to identify our discipline's threshold concepts and build our courses around students' attaining them. Students will have to engage in critical thinking by comparing information and experimental results to their misguided theories. If they find they cannot defend their ideas to their peers, that the evidence in front of them is too compelling to ignore, then they may correct their worldview. When they can explain the correct theory and apply it instead of their incorrect one, they have changed their worldview permanently.

We, too, tend to resist when faced with new ideas. We, like so many others, prefer the comfortable known. You may experience some resistance to new ideas as you read this book. But please persist, because the insights are crucial to good teaching, and once you try them, you won't want to go back.

I wasn't on this journey alone. A group of teacher innovators at my school got interested in these ideas, too, and we became a learning community, sharing our triumphs and failures as we experimented our way to better teaching. We had fun figuring out together how to read our students' thinking process, how to design better lessons, how to encourage students to be more independent in creating theories of their own.

This book attempts to introduce more teachers to the exciting findings in learning and cognition that our group has found so useful and inspiring, and to share some of the successful changes we made in our teaching. The book is primarily for high school teachers and the examples come from high school teachers, but the concepts can be adapted to younger classes as well. I hope the ideas will be like Lasik surgery for your teaching.

Carole Hamilton, 2015

Preface 1.1. We still design most lessons based on nineteenth century misconceptions of how students learn. Now we can design them based on exciting new principles from twenty-first century cognitive science!
Credit: Composite by Ned Hamilton, used with permission. Classroom painting "The Village School in 1848," by Albert Anker, Kunstmuseum Basel, public domain. From the-athenaeum.org

Acknowledgments

With much gratitude to and respect for my colleagues who share a passion for pedagogy: Robert Coven, Matt Greenwolfe, Ned Hamilton, Heidi Maloy, Palmer Seeley, German Urioste, and Troy Weaver. And many thanks to Sanje Ratnavale for his insights, suggestions, and support.

Introduction

> Classrooms are too often places of "tell and practice." The teacher tells the students what is important to know or do and then has them practice that skill or knowledge. In such classrooms, little thinking is happening. Teachers in such classrooms are rightly stumped when asked to identify the kinds of thinking they want students to do because there isn't any to be found in much of the work they give students. Retention of information through rote practice isn't learning: it is training. (Ritchhardt, Church, and Morrison 2011, 3)

Recent findings from cognitive science hold a lot of promise for teachers because we now have a clearer idea of how people learn. With these insights, we can, and should, teach differently to capitalize on this knowledge. This book describes three important new principles from cognitive science about how students learn that underscore the need to revolutionize our way of teaching. We must move away from the mode of giving students information, to one of helping them learn to think like practitioners in our disciplines. These principles actually work. I have tried them, and I have seen how effective they have been in other classrooms.

Here are the principles; when implemented together, they transform learning to be more effective and durable:

- We need to teach in a way that efficiently puts new information and the logic that holds it together into the brain. Our brains store information in categories that we make by noticing analogies, so we need to tap into that storage mechanism.
- We need to design lessons that cause students to learn for themselves. Students learn best when they figure things out, rather than being told or drilled.
- We need to cause students to confront their misperceptions and conquer the threshold concepts in our disciplines that are central to understanding.

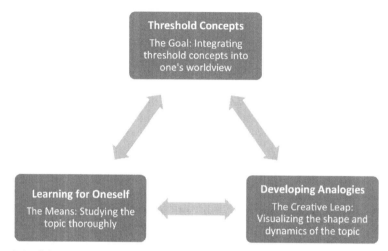

Intro I.1.

Every day, we teachers pick up the bow of education, grab an arrow out of the quiver of teaching methods, aim at the target, and very often miss. We miss not only the target of better scores, but, more importantly, we miss the target of teaching students how to think in our disciplines, to move toward a level of competency as future scientists, readers, historians, mathematicians. Of course, this is a huge generalization, and of course many teachers successfully imbue their students with the knowledge and wisdom they need. But, in general, too many teachers work far too hard for the amount of durable learning that occurs in their classes.

The main problem is that when teachers pick up that bow, they are already misinformed about how people learn in the first place, so their methods, including the latest trends, rarely match up with how students need to be taught. Thus, when planning where to focus, what to teach, how to teach, and how to assess, they are not taking into account how human brains actually learn, and they are off target from the start. Even lessons wrapped in technology or the souvenirs of the latest conference are really old wine poured into new bottles. Since we are not achieving the results we want, why do we continue teaching essentially the same way we always have, while students remain mostly oblivious of the learning we think they are absorbing?

Not only is education itself in a crisis, we must also consider the effects of inadequate learning on our society. At what cost do we push students along the conveyor belt of rote performance in school, barely interrupting their attention on the technical gadgets that fill their time and drive the economy? Students who haven't learned to think, even those with high scores on standardized tests, enter the workforce as drones willing to accept assignments without question and to fulfill them obediently, without fully considering any deleterious ethical and environmental impacts of their work. This is a willed oblivion that we engender, in the service of a society that continues to strip away the dignity and the remuneration of teachers.

Furthermore, because most of our students drift into citizenship with untested critical thinking skills, they have little ability to make head or tail of our complex and problem-fraught society, and thus fall victim to misinformation and false rhetoric. Even when we teach units on social problems and try to raise their consciousness, we merely alert them to reality; we do not equip them with the tools they need to fight those problems.

This impact on society exists because students who fail to master the critical concepts in our disciplines are not able to go out in the world and use them. We teachers play a key role in a vicious circle of deadening curiosity, dampening thought, and routinizing performance. If we want to change things, our teaching methods will need a serious overhaul, not a mechanization of what we already do, by taping lectures or finding online lessons for students to watch. We need to go back to the drawing board, remind ourselves what the teaching enterprise should be about, and make some important changes.

There are no easy fixes to problems this big, but because of recent findings in cognitive science and empirical studies of how students learn, we now have important and exciting solutions that can help us teach far more effectively. We not only can genuinely teach students how to think critically in our disciplines, but we can inspire their confidence and passion for thinking and authentic learning. If we do so, our students will become the kind of citizens who can take on our society's problems with confidence, competence, and zeal.

First we should ask, "What would we do if other human enterprises were not producing good enough results?" In a simple analogy, what would a mechanic do if a car continued to stall? Would he resort to a new idea he read about on another mechanic's blog, or tell the car owner he just isn't trying hard enough, or create a bank of tests on the tire inflation, braking time, and the coolness of the air conditioning? Or would he rather go straight to looking under the hood to see the engine working? Auto mechanics are practical people, just like teachers, so they prefer to zero in on the problem itself. They don't want to waste time on fads or ineffective chores. They will look under the hood.

At last, teachers, too, can "look under the hood" of their students' learning engine to see their thinking and how to fix it. Ten years ago, "brain science" was all about neurons and brain scans. Not useful for teachers. But today we have substantial empirical evidence from cognitive scientists that explains how humans think and learn; they have "read" the mind and understand how learning takes place. We teachers can also learn to read our students' minds to assess how they are thinking. That's where we must start. With all we know now about how brains learn, no teacher should have to consider a single new "souvenir from a conference" teaching method until she understands how students learn best and how the new method fits in with what we know about the brain's learning process.

Intro I.2.

Currently, the information from cognitive science and empirical studies about learning is scattered in different places, and few have managed to pull it together in the interest of better teaching. This book attempts to rectify that by providing a brief and clear overview of three of the most exciting findings (that we learn through analogy, that processing information oneself and developing theories creates durable learning not rote learning, and that the core threshold concepts of a discipline are central to becoming a practitioner). These insights can lead to better teaching and learning. Thus the book begins with an explanation of how learning occurs, which is through experience and interacting with the world, not by being told or drilled, and developing new and revised categories and analogies as we grow and learn.

Cognitive scientists tell us that, as new situations occur, a key component of creating understanding comes from a process of comparing and making analogies to what is already known. Therefore, the section on analogy provides the logic behind the idea of "analogy as the core of cognition" and many examples. After a quick review of some common traditional teaching methods that do not work as well as teachers hope, the book describes some highly effective new teaching methods that take advantage of what we now know about how students learn best. The third principle, regarding threshold concepts, provides a means to design courses around the most important values and ideas of a given discipline, the concepts that inspire and drive practitioners. The shift in teaching approach leads to a reenvisioning of how we assess students. This book suggests prioritizing analysis of *how students think* over *what they know*, so it explains how to make that shift, giving many examples. There are three main sections in the book, corresponding to the three theories of (1) thinking by analogy, (2) causing students to face misconceptions and create their own knowledge, and (3) identifying and integrating threshold concepts more meaningfully. The appendices contain relevant quotations to spark curiosity to learn more, sources for further reading, and sample ideas from teachers who have begun to implement the concepts described here.

I

HOW STUDENTS LEARN BEST

Children begin in preschool years to develop sophisticated understandings (whether accurate or not) of the phenomena around them. Those initial understandings can have a powerful effect on the integration of new concepts and information. Sometimes those understandings are accurate, providing a foundation for building new knowledge. But sometimes they are inaccurate. In science, students often have misconceptions of physical properties that cannot be easily observed. In humanities, their preconceptions often include stereotypes or simplifications, as when history is understood as a struggle between good guys and bad guys. A critical feature of effective teaching is that it elicits from students their preexisting understanding . . . and provides opportunities to build on—or challenge—the initial understanding. (Donovan, Bransford, and Pellegrino 2000, 10–11)

Learning starts when, as infants, we explore the physical world. While crawling around, seeing, exploring, touching, feeling textures, overcoming obstacles, and playing with toys, babies build an initial framework of the laws of physics, discovering that, for example, a tower of blocks topples easily, that pushing over a stack of books takes more effort. In each of their physical encounters with the world, they build the rudiments of physics concepts such as force, although they don't get the full picture. Physics teachers explain that children "learn it wrong" because although children grow up in a world of friction, they don't perceive it operating.

When children push a toy across a floor and it eventually slows down, they think their pushing it was the only factor. Thus, their model of force becomes "a body has velocity only when I am pushing on it." They have created a category, or mental schema, or map, of how force works, and that schema gets used daily as the child interacts with the world. When the schema's predictions work, this reinforces its usefulness. Since most children can navigate their world without learning about friction, they carry this incorrect model, or schema, into their high school physics classes. As they grow, they add more chunks of information and adopt other categories and schemas that may be inaccurate or incomplete. It is our job as teachers to help them root out the misconceptions and build more accurate schemas.

As learning continues, categories, schemas, and chunks of knowledge multiply and get confirmed or adjusted. As the child experiences more moments when she can predict what will happen next, it gives her the satisfaction of confirming or improving her worldview. The child builds a number of theories about how things work, from blocks and train sets to getting attention and building relationships.

Furthermore, the satisfaction of confirming a theory through more experience leads children to seek additional opportunities to explore, theorize, and add to a growing network of ideas and schemas that make up their worldview, their theory of how the world works. When children (and all of us) face something new, they sift through their categories and schemas, comparing them to the new situation, deciding if any fit. In other words, they check to see if the new situation is analogous to one they already understand. If not, they work hard to figure out how much it differs and if it's worth adding a new category or schema for it. Children like to think.

We see this sifting process in ourselves, too. Imagine waking up in the middle of the night and seeing an unfamiliar shape. Our mind whirs into action, though not very efficiently because we are groggy: Is it a bear? But there are no ears. Or is that an ear? No. Then is it a person sitting there? Unlikely. Now we begin to wake up a bit. Oh, it's the pillow I put on the chair before I went to bed! Back to sleep.

In seeing a creature walking through the yard, instantly a series of template possibilities race through the mind, searching for a fit. A cat? Too large. A fox? Wrong color. A dog? Too scruffy. A coyote? Are there coyotes in North Carolina? The mind resists this last idea and goes back to the dog or fox. The template of the fox seems to "color" the animal reddish, even though the animal is too tall for a fox and is a dirty cream color. So the color fades back to reality, a dingy cream color. Now wavering between dog and coyote, the viewer has to admit that it sure looked like a coyote.

When a neighbor mentions having seen it, too, and is confident that it was a coyote, the mind opens up to the possibility that, yes, coyotes do exist in North

"People like to think—or more properly, we like to think if we judge that the mental work will pay off with the pleasurable feeling we get when we solve a problem. So there is no inconsistency in claiming that people avoid thought and in claiming that people are naturally curious—curiosity prompts people to explore new ideas and problems, but when we do, we quickly evaluate how much mental work it will take to solve the problem. If it's too much or too little, we stop working on the problem if we can." (Willingham 2010, 13)

Carolina. What the viewer's mind did when she saw something that didn't click immediately was to try out various categories, noting anomalies and trying again when the anomalies made the fit imperfect. This is a process we enact daily, throughout our lives (What was that noise? Is that a mouse?), and we often try to force a fit and resist options that seem to us unlikely or impossible.

Students, having fewer life experiences, rarely notice anomalies in their understanding. They often accept what we would consider a sloppy fit, and only a dose of reality will lead them to change their minds. Into every one of their classes, they carry their misperceptions about how the world works, and in too many cases, they advance to the next grade carrying those exact same misconceptions, despite having been "taught" the right way to perceive their misconceptions.

Students (and people in general) can be very resistant to changing their minds, even with the truth before them. It takes mental work and genuine engagement to process the new perspective earnestly, such that the truth before the students begins to ring true for them. Therefore, they need to conduct more experimentation and exploration to achieve accuracy.

In school, when students encounter the correct view of physics, we hope they will transform their worldview according to the more sophisticated understanding. In fact, we assume that an explanation, an experiment, and a test will do the trick. Disappointingly, however, most students (even those who ace the exam) do not essentially alter their internal understanding with the new knowledge. They resist it.

In place of actual learning, they superficially memorize the new data for the class, without taking the time to reconcile their preestablished worldview with what they have "learned." They see "stuff I know" and "stuff I have to learn" as two separate arenas, because they haven't been required to reconcile them. And because their initial schemas are strong and well embedded, the students simply parrot the new information for the exam and continue to fall back on their trusty, inaccurate, schemas in their life. Just as truth bows to belief, it's easier to revert to learned schemas and ignore the poor fit than to revise them according to reality. Real thinking is hard.

To overcome students' natural resistance to changing their worldview, we have to design lessons that cause students to confront the anomalies and try to make sense of them so that they can revise their misperceptions. This requires taking a completely different approach to the work we do with our students. It means more problem solving and less rote learning. It means more time making observations and practicing critical thinking, and less time cramming facts.

> "When we can get away with it, we don't think. Instead we rely on memory. Most of the problems we face are ones we've solved before, so we just do what we've done in the past." (Willingham 2010, 6)

1

We Learn through Analogies

Categorization is actually the core [of cognition, and] analogy is the motor of the car of thought. (Hofstadter 2006)

Our minds store information in "chunks" of ideas and experience. If we organize those chunks into schemas, or meaningful frameworks, that information will be easier to retrieve and more long lasting. Schemas get built through analogical thinking— comparing new situations to known ones, looking for similarities. The schema is a category of things that we understand or recognize. We all have a huge category for animals, for example, and inside that category, smaller categories for types of animals, such as domestic, wild, predatory, game, species, and the like. We also have categories for actions, emotions, landscapes, driving rules, and so on.

According to cognitive scientist Douglas Hofstadter, each time we approach a novel situation, our minds try to fit it into a category that we already understand. If it fits, then the new situation is just another example of category x. If it doesn't fit any of our preestablished categories, then we may have to create a new one. In sifting through existing categories and creating new ones, we use analogical thinking as the mechanism to compare essential traits to see if they match. If they do not, we decide whether to create a new category. The whole time we are conscious, we sift through our categories, revising, adding, and making connections between them.

Many cognitive scientists assert that all learning is accomplished through analogy, starting initially with "chunks" of learned idea blocks that get expanded and refined into schemas through processing analogous and novel situations. There may be lots of "chunks" within the analogy, a full concept network of traits, examples, counter-examples, and connections to other blocks and schemas.

When the schema takes on an identity through an analogy, it becomes very easy to retrieve. Hofstadter, in his Presidential Lecture at Stanford University, gives the example of an airline hub, which has many related chunks, such as airlines and their tickets, rules, schedules, and flight plans, and also the food and consumer products in the waiting areas.

The concept of a "hub" derives from the idea of a ball that rolls, thence to a wheel, which brings in the concepts of spokes, centrality, and, finally, a hub. There are many more connections to the airport hub, strings, including trip, destination, a leg of a trip, the route, and so on, and these also connect across other concept strings to concepts such as schedules, networks, and timetables. The word *hub* is just one of millions of complex networks of chunks with many interrelating concepts that we can access from various points that connect within or to another concept map.

We have an unlimited capacity to add new chunks, new categories, new analogies, and new connections. However, all of the chunks do not come rushing into our minds at once when we retrieve an analogy. The analogy serves as a sort of shorthand concept that can be probed but doesn't need to be. When we talk with other people, we use shorthand words all the time: concepts such as a *frontrunner, spam, hashtag, burn out, failed state, consumer addict, keeping up with the Joneses, ethnic cleansing, the Big Gulp, sidestepping a problem, budding actress, man cave, casualties of war, soul-sucking meetings*; the list goes on.

Hofstadter asks how many levels of structure we would have to explain for someone from two thousand years ago to fully understand the word *Wikipedia*. The underlying concepts include computers, the Internet, Wi-Fi, encyclopedias, freedom of information, open collaboration, real-time updates, and more. Our minds keep all of these chunks organized and ready to retrieve, but we don't always need all of the details because the analogy conveys the essence of the thought. We can sift through the chunks (and chunks within chunks) of information when we need to.

Categories, schemas, and analogies all refer to the structures learning creates in the brain, but the word *analogy* (which can also be a metaphor or simile) includes the added feature of a vivid and memorable label. For example, the phrase *congressional gridlock* is a metaphor that conjures up an image of representatives not moving forward, not agreeing, but getting in each other's way; perhaps the analogy conjures up the image in our mind's eye of a gridlocked traffic intersection.

We also carry in our minds simple schemas, such as brushing one's teeth or following the roadmaps in our minds that tell us how to get to work. These schemas do not need a vivid analogy; we automatically employ the maps without having to think about them. Some schemas are simple and straightforward, such that they guide us

> "When you feel as though you are 'on autopilot,' even if you're doing something rather complex, such as driving home from school, it's because you are using memory to guide your behavior. Using memory doesn't require much of your attention, so you are free to daydream, even as you're stopping at red lights, passing cars, watching for pedestrians, and so on." (Willingham 2010, 7)

seeming automatically. Others have lots of subideas or chunks, and these come to us as a clear concept, leaving all the details out of our mind until we decide to probe them to retrieve more information. The information will be well organized if the person thoughtfully processed it and created a meaningful analogy.

Analogies clarify concepts efficiently because certain characteristics and traits of the analogy or metaphor "map" onto the traits of the target, giving shape and form to what otherwise would be a mass of unorganized data. Our first analogies come from the physical world, when as children we explored, made observations, drew conclusions, and compared new situations to experienced ones. Because our initial experiences were visual and tactile, many of our most effective analogies are visual or tactile. In fact, 30 percent of our brain neurons are dedicated to vision, while hearing gets only 3 percent. No wonder so many analogies are visual. It's also worth remembering that potentially only 3 percent of our students' brains are engaged when we lecture in class!

Hofstadter cites numerous examples of effective visual analogies and also demonstrates how they tend to create other spinoff analogies to fit other circumstances. For example, he mentions how the noun *shadow* has spawned analogies such as *snow shadow*—the space under a tree where the snow doesn't fall through to the ground, leaving a snowless area—and the *rain shadow*—the arid region to the east of some mountain ranges—as well as the phrase *he's always been in her shadow*, and we can add the phrase *five o'clock shadow*.

These visual analogies create an instant image in our minds that facilitates communication and understanding. Tactile analogies (which require about 8 percent of the brain) are also effective. Consider the almost physical sensation of reading these commonly used metaphors: *She sure sucker punched him, My feet are like lead*, and *She took my breath away.*

Figure 1.1.

Here's another example. We might say, "She cast her mind back to 1995." The word *cast*, which is strongly associated with fishing, evokes an underlying metaphor, that of the mind as a receptacle or pool of memories. One casts one's line into the lake to see what can be caught. The metaphor works well because of the indeterminacy of what will be caught or recalled: in fishing, we don't know what we'll catch, and when daydreaming about the past, we can't predict what memories will surface. Thus the traits of cast fishing map onto the traits of memory recall, helping to explain how this kind of recall happens.

Along the same lines, the metaphor of a *pool shark* maps onto a skilled pool player the traits of a predator comfortable in his own surroundings, able to approach with stealth, and eager to consume the unwary pool player. All metaphors transfer traits to the "target" idea, influencing the way we process and value it. In some ways, metaphors simplify the concept and can even, at times, skew it.

But a vivid analogy or metaphor is memorable and easy to recall, and the schema holds information in an organized way that makes retrieval efficient. Learned nuances also get organized into the schema efficiently so that the mind contains as much information as needed. By comparison, memorized information that hasn't been structured into an analogy can float rather aimlessly in the mind and easily become forgotten.

A good analogy is memorable and stays with us. Sigmund Freud's metaphors and analogies of the human psyche have stuck despite the fact that many of the theories themselves no longer hold true. He spoke of the mind as an "apparatus" or a "steam engine," the id as a "cauldron of seething excitement," and the ego as subservient to the "three harsh masters" of the "external world, the super-ego, and the id."

The emphasis on mechanical metaphors comes from the industrial age in which Freud lived. People were fascinated by the new machinery and factory processes being invented and changing the economy. The source image (seething cauldron, steam engine) transfers traits of power, constancy, and energy onto the subject, the brain.

Similarly, when computer technology burst onto the scene, many psychologists began to apply the metaphor of computer systems to the mind. Now the mind had traits of being programmable and of always processing data. Analogies hold a lot of power: Freud's analogy of family dynamics as a version of the Oedipus story remains compelling. We also use analogies every day, when we speak ("She sure is down today"), process something new ("Is that a spider or a piece of lint?"), or try to

> "Cognitive scientists have identified metaphors as a fundamental tool of human thought; we use metaphors so frequently and automatically that we seldom notice them unless they are called to our attention. Metaphors are used to structure our experience and thereby make it meaningful. A major objective of teaching should therefore be to help students 'straighten out' their metaphors." (Jackson, Dukerich, and Hestenes 2008, 13)

convey a thought succinctly and vividly ("It was like a bomb went off in my brain"). It's how we think.

Our brains are constantly comparing new situations with established categories and concept chunks, and these comparisons, these attempts to find shared essential traits, can happen rapidly, in seconds. A reviewer of this book suggested that in this section the process of analogy making may have been oversimplified in the interest of clarity. This prompted an immediate thought: "Lard in some more." The thought came instantaneously: it injected itself into my mind.

Larding is a cooking term for injecting fat into a piece of overly lean meat to make it juicier. The reviewer had suggested that the discussion of analogies was too "lean," so it was necessary to add a bit of "fat," including this paragraph. Larding is easy, a reassurance that the task would not become overwhelming.

As analogies pile up in our brains, we link them with other, related or comparable schemas and chunks of understanding. The creating, storing, mapping, and retrieving of categories, schemas, analogies, and concept chunks make up human cognition. This is learning.

Children are wired to learn. But they are not wired to learn by rote memorization. They learn by building schemas and associating new concepts and information to them. Unfortunately, too many of our teaching methods fail to engage students' minds in assessing situations against their storehouse of schemas that tell them how the world works, even though some of them may be incomplete or faulty. If, as Hofstadter says, "analogy is the core of cognition," then teachers would be well advised to modify their teaching approach so that students can create meaningful analogies that they can easily retrieve and process information in a way that stores it in the schema that the analogy creates in their brains.

If students have misperceptions (we all do!), then our lessons need to compel them to interrogate their view of how the world works with the information they process in our lessons. We cannot simply tell them what is right, though we often resort to that, along with the admonition that "This is important!" But what we tell them, no matter how urgently we insist, is not as compelling to our students as what they learn through experience. If we can engineer experiences for them, challenges that they have to grapple with and really think through, then there is hope that they will be able to change their misperceptions into more correct understandings of how the world works.

This approach also requires a different manner of assessment. Now we need to check on their thinking, not their ability to spit out the expected answer when called upon. Amazingly, students can hold onto their misperceptions while parroting the right answer on tests, without the twain ever meeting. So designing effective challenges that cause them to engage fully in ideas and learning how to assess the results in their thinking become of paramount importance.

If Hofstadter is correct in defining intelligence as "the ability to put one's finger on the essence of a situation rapidly . . . to categorize rapidly, to find compelling and strong analogies rapidly," then we as teachers can do a great service to our students by helping them sharpen their ability to categorize and develop analogies.

For further reading, see Appendix A, "How People Learn," and Appendix B, "Analogy as the Core of Cognition."

Summing up, so far we have considered new insights from cognitive science that reveal how people learn, which starts in babyhood and continues throughout our lives. We learn by analogy, by constantly comparing known categories of things, events, emotions, and language, always building new analogies and categories as we need them, and revising them when anomalies force us to reconsider what we think we already know. With the principle in mind that analogy is the core of cognition, we now examine some of our current teaching methods and how they stack up against this new insight. As it turns not, many do not stack up very well.

II

WHY MUCH OF OUR
TEACHING IS INEFFECTIVE

The key issue is less how to change, but why we do not. In a fascinating study, Shermer (1997) researched why we tend (often passionately) to believe in ideas even when they do not work. He attributed this to an over reliance on anecdotes, dressing up one's beliefs in the trappings of science or pedagogical language and jargon, making bold claims, relying on one's past experiences rather than others' experiences, claiming that one's own experience is sufficient evidence, and circular reasoning. (Hattie 2008, 252)

Unfortunately, few schools build upon the child's natural manner of acquiring knowledge. Unfortunately, too, teachers have been trained to think of their role as providers of information whose goal is to "fill up" the child's head with facts. Thus too many of our lessons involve lecture, passive reading, and cut-and-paste retrieval instead of engaging students in the theory making that allows them to integrate new information into their worldview. It's as though the student watches a school-day-long film of facts, a hodge-podge of information, with few opportunities to engage their learning machines, or to follow a natural process of discovery, theorizing, and revising their worldview.

When we tell the students the end product of thinking, rather than designing an opportunity for them to think themselves, we rob them of a precious opportunity to correct and expand their worldview. And slowly, the effect of disengagement with real learning erodes the desire to learn, because the blank-slate methodology is dull work compared to natural learning and therefore not satisfying to the student. But now that we understand how to harness the natural learning process, classrooms that offer no opportunity to explore—just to digest and memorize—represent tragic lost opportunities for effective teaching and learning. Instead, we must design opportunities for students to engage in real thinking so they can construct their own schemas and analogies.

This book does not suggest that no learning is happening at present, but we can accomplish much more by lecturing and drilling far less. And the learning can be more durable when we teach to the child's natural learning process and thus change not just what a student knows but how he or she thinks. One version of this style of teaching, called modeling instruction, accomplishes permanent, deep, transferable learning that has transformed thousands of physics classes into more successful educational experiences. It has also gained traction in chemistry and biology and is getting attention in the humanities as well.

What has drawn teachers to the method are studies that measure student retention of the key laws of physics. The studies show that when students grapple with data before being given formulas and they develop their own visual representations and theories about what is happening, their retention rate is double that of students taught by traditional methods. No matter how much the traditional teacher repeats the rules of physics, students systematically misunderstand them and continue to apply their own pre-Newtonian concepts to the experiments and homework problems.

In the studies, students in traditional classes averaged a 42 percent retention rate, while those in modeling instruction classes averaged 69 to 80 percent retention. This is because students in modeling classes face their misconceptions early on and develop their own visual representations of theories, processes, and forces. Once they develop visual representations of their theories, they can turn their attention to schema and analogy creation, which gives the information they learn a place to reside. They understand physics at a deep level of cognition, and they change their worldview to incorporate what they observe to be true.

See Appendix C, "Student Retention with Schemas and Analogies."

2

How We Should
(and Should Not) Teach

In the often-misunderstood notion of experiential or inquiry-based learning, students are sometimes provided with lots of activities. Again, if designed well some of these activities can lead to understanding, but too often the thinking that is required to turn activity into learning is left to chance. Other times, the activity itself is little more than a more palatable form of practice. Playing a version of Jeopardy to review for a test may be more fun than doing a worksheet, but it is still unlikely to develop understanding. (Ritchhardt, Church, and Morrison 2011, 32)

Education should be about transforming the way students think and elevating their view by pushing and guiding them through the most troublesome, challenging, and fundamental issues in each discipline. But there are more ineffective means of teaching being practiced today than effective ones. Direct instruction, lecturing, drill, and memorization do not work well because they encourage shallow memorization of facts and mechanical procedures. Yes, students do need to encounter a sufficient amount of discipline-specific content to build understanding, but students also need to build mental schemas to organize that information, to improve understanding and facilitate retrieval.

What has been termed "discovery learning" does not work because students all too easily wander through the intellectual landscape while avoiding the important yet troublesome and challenging areas that lead to transformation. Often, when teachers assign "discovery learning" assignments, they expect students to find their own sources, assess them for quality, and then discover something important. This approach lacks the guidance a teacher should give in selecting sources. It's as though the teacher abdicates her responsibility yet expects a brilliant insight from the student. With those kinds of stakes, students will try to find something provable. Better yet, they will find something already proven and then just build an essay or project around someone else's thinking.

Thus a teacher's guidance is needed to push students out of their comfort zones and make sure that the topics they explore really engage their critical thinking and lead to a confrontation with their misconceptions. Yes, it is true that a certain amount of open exploration is crucial for students to honestly assess their own pre-existing notions in order to compare them to those of other students and to their observations in class.

The art of effective teaching lies in choosing content and challenges that will target some common, specific notions and instigate genuine investigation. Teaching to how students learn requires architecting experiences that cause students to grapple directly with the central truths of the discipline. We will discuss those central truths in the section on threshold concepts.

For now, we can think of core or threshold concepts as the main values shared by those in the discipline, the beliefs and commitments made to uphold the ideals of that discipline. These are the values that draw people to the field in the first place and make it endlessly fascinating. Unfortunately, teachers often take these concepts for granted, assuming that experience with the skills and habits of a practitioner will lead students to understand them.

Simple collaboration group and project work are not effective because, left to their own devices, novices in a subject tend to focus on details and miss the overarching structure and order of ideas. Yet, through the style of collaboration found in modeling instruction, including deliberate conversation with peers about how things work (rather than what happened), each student's preexisting ideas get raised to consciousness and explicitly stated, compelling the student to improve his understanding and schemas.

Anyone trying to master a subject needs feedback on whether she is on the right path and making progress. But feedback through summative grades can atrophy a student's intrinsic motivation and may drive students to avoid deeper thought while parroting the desired answers.

To be more effective, teachers require a multidimensional view of the structure of students' knowledge and to understand how they are thinking through this knowledge, as opposed to assessing rote memorization and mechanical procedure. What we seek is a true transformation of their thought process. Therefore, students must express their ideas using multiple modes—spoken word and presentation, writing, diagrams, graphs, and other visuals. Assessment systems must be redesigned to encourage students to pursue continual growth, not close down thought, as often happens when a grade marks the end of the learning.

By challenging students' preconceived notions and structuring lessons so students develop their own theories and modify their worldview, teachers can teach to the way that students learn best. So how do we do that? It requires a reenvisioning of teaching, which calls for deep critical thinking on our part as we reconsider the basic goals of the course and then reorient our lessons around the key concepts of the discipline. It also requires a change in teaching methods to make sure students grapple with those ideas. Of the teacher, it requires a different teaching style and different ways of assessing student performance.

In this section, we learned that many traditional ways of teaching do not necessarily cause students to embrace and adopt new ways of thinking, and in fact students often resist learning new ideas because it is far easier to rely on their current perspective and memories than to do the deep thinking to revise or correct it. Thus many students keep two versions of the topic: one that is embedded in their worldview and one that is memorized for the course (i.e., for the test), and afterwards the new learning is abandoned.

We need to engage the students' natural way of learning—encountering reality and becoming interested enough to test it against current theories—so that they begin to think like a practitioner in our discipline. The next section addresses this, first by explaining the natural learning style, then by addressing the standard questions each teacher faces when designing a course—where to focus, what to teach, how to teach, how to assess—to see what changes to make in each.

III

TEACHING TO THE STUDENT'S NATURAL LEARNING STYLE

Here's the problem. Currently, we approach planning this way:

- Where to Focus: Decide on a theme or area of emphasis, often dictated by external standards.
- What to Teach: Choose texts and topics.
- How to Teach: Use lectures, assigned readings, class discussions, and so on.
- How to Assess: Give tests, quizzes, and essay or project assignments.

With a better understanding of how people think and learn, we can change our approach and address the same four questions more productively:

- Where to Focus: Identify threshold concepts and organize the course around them.
- What to Teach: Choose texts and topics that exemplify threshold concepts.
- How to Teach: Design lessons that compel students to confront their misperceptions.
- How to Assess: Design ways to gauge students' critical thinking process in the discipline.

Each of the revised steps is addressed next. Although the concepts in these sections may seem simple, they take time and thought to deploy. The payoff comes when they get implemented together, for they can lead to a dramatic improvement in students' critical thinking.

As teachers reorient their courses to correspond with how people learn best, students will be more satisfied and teachers will enjoy a less labor-intensive and more reflective and productive practice. Often the same materials can be used, and some of the lessons can remain the same but with a "flipped" approach.

Now we approach the lessons knowing that we want students to discover threshold concepts on their own. This means presenting students with challenges and giving them the materials and means to figure out those threshold concepts. Threshold concepts are the governing ideas of a discipline, and self-learning that leads to making useful analogies is the means to discover those governing ideas.

You will notice that skills haven't been mentioned. Of course we must teach skills: skills in reading insightfully, writing clearly, using lab equipment safely, creating and interpreting graphs accurately, and the like. We already know to give students time to practice, practice, practice, to give helpful feedback, to space out practice sessions instead of trying to inculcate skills all at once, and to make sure they know when to use them and why they are important. So this book will not spend a lot of time on the teaching of skills, but know that skills can feel like thresholds for students, too, in that they must enter a foreign territory and gain confidence in their abilities with a skill set that will initially feel clumsy and off-putting.

Once again, they will try to just get the job done quickly, whereas we want them to enjoy the process and take ownership of the quality of their work. Our role is to help them take pride in mastering the skills as key steps in becoming a practitioner in the discipline. Anyone who has walked into a biology or physics classroom and seen students totally immersed in measuring, observing, graphing, drawing, and conferring seriously with their peers about their findings knows how rewarding it can be to inspire students to savor the daily routines of our disciplines and to want to excel at them (see Appendix E, "Sample Threshold Concepts and Skills").

Now let's look in detail at the revised stages of planning.

3

Where to Focus

Identify Threshold Concepts

A threshold concept is conceived in a quite different way [from other course learning]. From the point of view of the expert, it is an idea which gives shape and structure to the subject, but it is inaccessible to the novice. In fact, it may be counter-intuitive in nature and off-putting. It can appear to be a denial of the world which the student experiences and it may therefore lead to the student rejecting the subject as "abstract" and "meaningless." (Meyer and Land 2006, 75)

The first area of focus is the most challenging but the most crucial to success. The teacher needs to identify the roughly seven to ten key concepts in the course. These will take the form of statements of truth that a master in the field would consider foundational. Unfortunately, most masters, teachers included, know these truths intuitively rather than explicitly, so it can be quite difficult to identify them.

For example, in English classes, we want students to write essays that explore a topic and not simply offer a pat and boring summary. But we seldom give students opportunities to discover this idea in class, and even more rarely teach students explicitly how to explore an idea versus simply make a claim and then prove it. And yet we rather perversely hold them accountable for a concept that we have not taught them or allowed them to discover. How unfair!

Other threshold concepts include "Poems hold competing ideas in eternal conflict," "Beliefs can overwhelm and distort facts," and "The interplay of homeostasis and equilibrium produces both constancy and dynamism in organisms." Such simple, true, statements that are obvious to practitioners are often counterintuitive to novices. Before continuing with how to organize a course around threshold concepts, we'll need to know what they are.

WHAT ARE THRESHOLD CONCEPTS?

According to Ray Land and Jan Meyer, threshold concepts are the central, defining truths in a given discipline, the ideas that open a gateway to deeper understanding. These are the essential, indispensable elements, the understandings that transform the novice into a true practitioner of the field. Experts consider someone who fails to grasp the threshold concepts of a discipline not to be a legitimate practitioner, to remain outside of the discipline. Unfortunately, because these ideas are not part of their worldview, students find them difficult, even counterintuitive, and so they actively resist learning them.

As cognitive science has shown us, humans invariably prefer to revert back to known schemas and resist testing or considering new theories. Our students cannot always hear or appreciate all of what we teach them because their faulty internal schemas "filter out" key parts of our message. They "systematically misunderstand" what we say to them (these terms come from David Hestenes, a pioneer of modeling instruction in physics) because their schemas do not match up with reality and the worldview that we take for granted.

They might ignore us or substitute an easier idea or some rote learning in order to avoid having to challenge their beliefs. Of course, what they barely grasp is not long retained. However, we can aid students in developing correct schemas and pertinent

Figure 3.1.
Credit: "Overcoming Student Barriers to Understanding PPT," Ray Land, used with permission.

analogies so that they understand and embed threshold concepts and are then able to retrieve and analyze information efficiently and accurately.

Often, teachers assess student work for evidence of understanding threshold concepts intuitively without explicitly discussing or prioritizing them in class. This creates frustration for both students and teachers. And even if the teacher explains these concepts and tests the students on them, the students may not integrate them into their worldview. But when we can engage students in exploring situations that force them to approach threshold concepts, it can change their way of thinking: they begin to think more like practitioners in the discipline than like novices. They begin to see important implications of the concept that enrich their understanding.

In fact, once threshold concepts are understood, once students pass through that gateway of understanding, there is no going back to prior beliefs. The corrected concept has embedded itself in the student's worldview. For example, economics students who grasp the concept of externalities change their perception of what "cost" really means. History students who discover that history is not progressive look at current events differently because they see the cyclical nature of conflict, the wider implications of wars and political impasses.

For those students who get hooked on biology, environmental science, math, history, English, and so on, it's the beauty and integrity of the cohesive design of that discipline, the elegance and potential for deep understanding of our world, that hooks them, and this does not occur just because the student ran a bunch of experiments, memorized some formulas, read a lot of well-written books, watched some exciting demonstrations, or felt riveted by a teacher's lectures. That's why we don't want to simplify and demystify our lessons, but rather to remystify them, to make them appealing and intriguing. Why drain the color from the sky?

Our students' insights come when they engage in the compelling problems of the discipline and discover the threshold concepts with which they resonate and accept as truths. They begin to develop the urge to spend time with and to explore those truths and the related concepts that make up the body of the discipline's knowledge and wisdom. Their exposure to critical thinking and teamwork awakens the desire to have more of these probing conversations, to learn from others, and to become knowledgeable enough to share insights with others, too.

> "Misconceptions can be entrenched and tend to be very resistant to instruction. . . . Hence, for concepts or theories in the curriculum where students typically have misconceptions, learning is more challenging. It is a matter of accommodation. Instead of simply adding to student knowledge, learning is a matter of radically reorganizing or replacing student knowledge. Conceptual change or accommodation has to occur for learning to happen. . . . Teachers will need to bring about this conceptual change." (Lucariello and Naff 2009)

When a student in an English class reads an innovative story, such as John Barthes "Lost in the Funhouse," David Foster Wallace's *Infinite Jest*, Dino Buzzati-Traverso's "The Falling Girl," Toni Morrison's *Beloved*, or Flannery O'Connor's "A Good Man Is Hard to Find," a thought may hit the student like a thunderbolt: "Writing can do this?" These writers break the rules: one narrator speaks directly to the reader and questions the turns of the plot as a plot; others include magical ideas innocently alongside realistic ideas or push reality to its limits. These refreshing, crazy, and incredibly appealing works can get students hooked on literature with one reading.

In the same way, a student of economics who discovers the principle of opportunity cost wants to shout it from the mountaintops; the student who discovers the Marxist theory of the inevitable moral bankruptcy of capitalist consumption wants to sell his designer sunglasses and work on a communal farm; the student who discovers the tremendous potential in medicine for vaccines decides to spend the rest of her life in the lab mesmerized by the wonders under the microscope. It's not just the information that cancer cells can be destroyed by targeted viruses; it is the threshold concept that life-forms can be altered to improve our chances of survival. It's not the idea of conservation alone that hooks the future river keeper, but the hope that her effort will help restore the river to its original pristine beauty.

The student in an English class does not turn to literary studies because he read a few well-written books, but because he has accepted into his worldview the threshold concept that writers offer wisdom for the human soul and that the great books engage meaningfully with the charged topics of their times. Math students don't turn to mathematics degrees just because they like solving polynomials, but because they see that math explains the beauty of nature. For true practitioners, these aren't just the icing on the cake—they are the cake, the reason they commit their lives to the disciplines.

Another way to consider threshold concepts is to consider which ideas seem very obvious to the teacher but which students are frustratingly slow to incorporate into their thinking. If it takes multiple iterations and an excessive amount of time to convey a concept the teacher considers as defining and central to the discipline, then it's probably a threshold concept.

So the first step to revitalizing our classes is to create a list of the threshold concepts from our discipline that we want students to integrate into their worldview. Remarkably, most disciplines have not identified the threshold concepts that lie at

"Difficulty in understanding threshold concepts may leave the learner in a state of 'liminality', a suspended state of partial understanding, or 'stuck place', in which understanding approximates to a kind of 'mimicry' or lack of authenticity. Insights gained by learners as they cross thresholds can be exhilarating but might also be unsettling, requiring an uncomfortable shift in identity, or, paradoxically, a sense of loss." (Meyer, Land, and Baillie 2010, x) their heart and inspire their practitioners. So in most cases teachers will have to ferret them out for themselves.

Here are some sample threshold concepts from various disciplines. Aren't these the kinds of ideas we want students to embrace?

- Beliefs can overwhelm and distort facts.
- There is a tragic disconnect between who benefits from and who pays for the environmental damage in our world.
- Opportunity cost, or the cost of forgoing a different choice, is the real cost of any decision and must be factored into decision making.
- In bioenergetics (photosynthesis and respiration), energy is not created or lost, just transformed.
- Societies (and individuals) define themselves in opposition to an "other."

In developing a list of threshold concepts, it can help to explain them to someone outside of the discipline. A person who is naïve about the discipline can ask clarifying questions to tease out the concepts that seem simple and obvious to a practitioner. The colleague needs to be tenacious and redirect the conversation so that it doesn't divert to explaining what and how the material is taught. The goal instead is to identify the concepts that have been invisible to the class and that students too often fail to grasp despite multiple lessons.

Once identified and refined, threshold concepts tend to be remarkably clear and simple. It is important to note that many threshold concepts are specific to a discipline. They derive from, and represent the basis of, that discipline. They organize our thoughts. They can also help us as practitioners to ignite the passion of our students for our discipline, by allowing them to see how these core ideas contain the heart of the discipline. We do our students a great service when we facilitate their ability to organize their ideas in a way similar to the way we do. It is better than stuffing them with facts and hoping that the organizing will occur spontaneously. It probably won't.

With a list of threshold concepts in hand, teachers can decide how to sequence the course and begin to consider which kinds of lessons will best lead the students to discover the threshold concepts themselves. Throughout the school year, this list can

> "The fact that experts' knowledge is organized around important ideas or concepts suggests that curricula should also be organized in ways that lead to conceptual understanding. Many approaches to curriculum design make it difficult for students to organize knowledge meaningfully. Often there is only superficial coverage of facts before moving on to the next topic; there is little time to develop important, organizing ideas. History texts sometimes emphasize facts without providing support for understanding. . . . Many ways of teaching science also overemphasize facts." (Bransford, Brown, and Cocking 2000, 42)

be refined as we discover which of the concepts were easy for students to grasp and which proved more challenging.

Does it make sense to begin with the simpler concepts, or is there an overarching concept that will make some of the others easier to identify? Are some too obvious or too sophisticated for your students? Analyzing the effectiveness of threshold concepts is an interesting process of critical thinking in itself.

See Appendix D for more on threshold concepts. For sample threshold concepts and skills from various courses, see Appendix E.

Now that we more fully understand threshold concepts, we can address the next stage of course planning, choosing materials.

4

What to Teach

Choose Topics and Texts That Exemplify Threshold Concepts

> Children have real understanding only of that which they invent themselves, and each time that we try to teach them something too quickly, we keep them from reinventing it themselves. (Jean Piaget, quoted in *Time* 1999)

Having identified the main threshold concepts, it becomes apparent that the course must be organized around attaining them. This might mean replacing some reading materials with texts that more explicitly make the key points.

Many of our units will work with this new style of teaching, but some will not. We will need to resequence lessons and shift the focus from, for example, the book–essay cycle in literature classes or the causes–event–consequences cycle in history classes to a pattern that starts with a challenge related to a threshold concept and provides sources that allow students to work their way to sophisticated understanding of the context as well as the knowledge, changing their worldview in the process. With this approach, some units might not fit in, and some will just need to be flipped to turn them into sources the student can explore in order to understand and solve the challenge problem, developing the actual skills a practitioner would use rather than trying to memorize information isolated from context.

Additionally, lessons and readings based solely on facts and dates will be less useful than texts that stimulate ideas and theories—texts that compel the student to grapple with why something happens, not just that it does or did. Students do need to process content—lots of it—but within the framework of learning threshold concepts to help organize the content in their minds. Factual knowledge is crucial, but it needs to be woven into a schema, not just dropped in raw. Basically, the old approach looks like figure 4.1. The new approach looks like figure 4.2.

Following are two examples, the first in the "conveyer belt" style and the second in the "challenge that leads to learning a threshold concept" style.

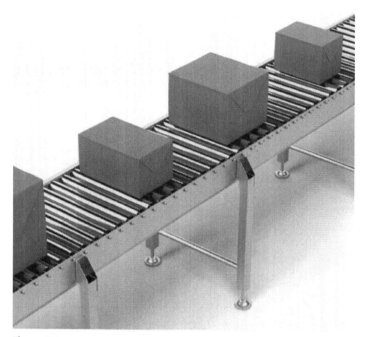

Figure 4.1.

The first teacher decides to teach the American Civil War by lecturing on the course of the war; describing key battles in detail; identifying key players such as Robert E. Lee, Ulysses S. Grant, Abraham Lincoln, and Jefferson Davis; discussing the war's impact on enslaved people; noting the human and material costs of the war; showing maps of the states as they aligned with the Union or Confederacy; explaining the point of "states' rights," and so on.

The lectures might be riveting, filled with gory sensory details and dramatic moments. The students take notes and follow the lectures with interest. They read the text for reinforcement, highlighting what they think are the important ideas. At the end of the unit, the students do fairly well on the test. However, a week later, they remember only scattered images and ideas. If they took the test again, they would not perform as well as the first time, when the details were fresher in their minds. They will have to restudy the material again for the final exam, along with all the other topics covered throughout the year. For the final exam, too, their recall will be scattered and their essay answers not as coherent as the teacher had hoped they would be.

The second teacher arranges the unit differently. She would like students to understand several threshold concepts relating to civil wars:

1. There is often a mismatch between intent and outcome that complicates the meaning and morality of historical decisions.
2. Societies (and individuals) define themselves in opposition to an "other."

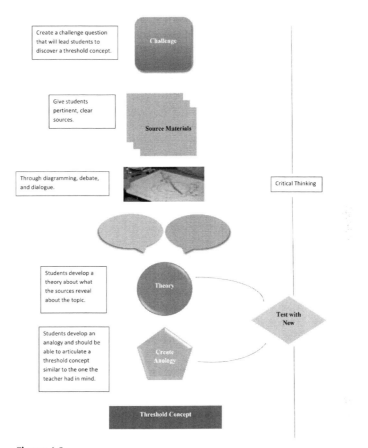

Figure 4.2.

3. There is a historical tension between the distribution and consolidation of resources and power.
4. Beliefs can overwhelm and distort facts.

For her unit, this teacher chooses events and people who clearly represent one or more of these threshold concepts. So, for threshold concept 1, she has students in groups analyze different key battles, asking them to explain why the outcomes occurred as they did and whether the overall goal of the battle was achieved. She doesn't need to lecture about the battles because the students can easily find animated troop movement maps, information about generals, death and injury statistics, and enough background information to put the battle into context.

Then she asks students to develop a theory about why some of the outcomes did not achieve the intended goals and whether the decisions were morally and ethically sound. She asks them to diagram the relationship between the planned and actual outcome and to come up with an analogy that fits their theory. Student groups present to the class their diagram, analogy, and theory along with the parts of their research that support it. They do not simply recount the details, stages, and statistics of a given battle but select pertinent information to back up their claims. This gives them good practice at creating and defending an argument efficiently and effectively.

Some may protest that this process takes too much time, that valuable information must be cut to allow students to process a few ideas deeply. This is a valid concern, but when one considers how little students remember overall, giving them the tools to organize their learning into retrievable units in their minds takes precedence over a few details overlooked. They would have forgotten them anyway. Knowing how to think critically in a given discipline will serve students better than cramming in more information because, once they think like a practitioner, they can anticipate how another, new idea might be structured and how it might operate in the world. By learning how to think, students gain more fluency and wisdom about the discipline itself.

Next, for threshold concepts 2, 3, and 4, the teacher has students read memoirs of former slaves, look at advertisements and bills of sale for slaves, analyze statistics on cotton production over time, find background information on the cotton industry in America and Britain, study prevailing notions of the personhood of enslaved peoples, find laws pertaining to escaped slaves, and look at maps showing the migration paths that slaves took from their homes in Africa to the tobacco fields of the Mid-Atlantic states and then down to the Southern cotton fields.

She asks them to explain how the enslavers managed to increase cotton production per slave year after year. She asks them to explain how the enslavers justified their treatment of African Americans. Why, for example, did the planters refuse to let their slaves attend African American churches? Why did the slaves not rise up and revolt? And when they did, what mechanisms blocked their success? If this sounds like a lot of work, it is time well spent, and a teacher can start with one unit, see how successful it is, then design more like it.

As the students research and discuss, their misconceptions about slavery will rise to the surface. Some may have the idea that the slaves did not revolt because they lacked courage and ambition; others may feel that the slaves should have learned a trade or how to read and write to make themselves more valuable, or that slaves had a pretty good deal since they had housing and food, access to medicine, and time to spend with their families after the workday ended. The students may hold these ideas but feel reluctant to admit them. The teacher can suggest that students discuss some of the general myths of slavery that their research has debunked rather than ask students to take ownership of opinions that they now realize are ill founded.

Again, after the students have researched their topic in depth, the teacher asks students to diagram their findings about the relationship between the enslaved and enslavers, including the forces, beliefs, and measures of control and influence over this relationship. They should also identify all the entities involved—not just the slaves and overseers, but also the slave traders, the laws, and the people not directly responsible for the situation (but who benefited from it).

As they draw, they discuss possible theories, each student defending his position and hearing the views of others. Eventually, they come to a consensus on the best theory they can develop. Then they devise an analogy that fits their theory. Students present to the rest of the class their diagram, analogy, and theory, along with the parts of their research that support it. They do not simply go into story-telling mode, but select pertinent information (laws, statistics, anecdotes) to back up their claims.

Each student in the group should be held accountable for explaining all of the evidence they use. They should not operate in "silo" mode, simply dividing up the work and each group member giving three separate presentations. Assessing their shared knowledge can be accomplished with a few well-aimed questions.

Their theory should approximate the threshold concepts the teacher wants them to learn even if they don't state them in the same terms. In general, it is best not to give the students the threshold concepts. By having students derive the concepts themselves, the ideas become more powerful and likely to change the students' worldview, thus making the threshold concept a permanent part of their value system.

If necessary, the teacher can ask general questions during the presentations to move students closer. Did the consequences of slavery match expectations (threshold concept 1)? How do people define themselves (2)? What happens to power in this historical example (3)? How can we account for the relationship between facts and belief in this situation (4)? These sophisticated questions require critical thinking to answer adequately. They also work as effective essay prompts, especially because they encourage students to organize their thoughts about what they learned.

Just from reading these contrasting approaches, you can easily decide which one will lead to better understanding and more durable learning. This is because the second teacher has activated students' critical thinking skills toward an achievable but challenging goal, provided access to pertinent and compelling information they can analyze, and asked questions to guide their inquiry but not lead them inevitably to a predetermined conclusion. The students might or might not ar-ticulate the threshold concepts exactly as the teacher has worded them, and might in fact come up with even more insightful conclusions. Either way, the theory is their own, the information has someplace to "stick," and their analogy will make retrieval much easier.

For example, a group of students might develop the analogy that trade in the In-dian Ocean is like a circuit, such that when political conflict occurs the circuit opens up and trade dwindles to a stop, but when the political climate is calm the circuit is closed and connected so that trade thrives. When students recall the analogy, they will recall related information with it. They will also retain what they learned because they figured it out themselves, changing their worldview in the process. They now understand the world better and will be more astute in analyzing situations that parallel what they discovered in this example.

Now, a short detour here, to ask, isn't this just constructivism?

Generally, yes, but in a more targeted version. It is constructivism aimed specifi-cally at developing critical thinking skills in the disciplines, and this book proposes a specific way of having students consolidate and present their findings.

The founder of constructivism, French philosopher Jean Piaget, believed that people naturally respond to their environment by building schemas that explain how the world works. As they grow and have new experiences, they create more schemas and build multiple connections between them as they assimilate more knowledge and accommodate their findings to reality. Lev Vygotsky added the notion of socialization to constructivism, positing that working with peers to solve problems enhances and deepens the learning experience.

Constructivism contains many benefits for learning. Constructivist teachers avoid lectures and telling in favor of having students explore a problem and propose solutions. The goal is to awaken their natural impulse to create their own knowledge. Often the students work in groups, design their own project plan, and decide on the product they will produce and be assessed on.

In the process of researching their project, students have to analyze information and fit it into a growing schema. It is important in constructivism that students discover truth themselves rather than be told. The teacher takes on the role of a guide, providing access to and suggestions for materials and posing Socratic questions, but essentially allowing students to operate fairly independently.

What Jean Piaget intuited about how people learn has now been proven true by cognitive science and empirical study. His principle that knowledge is created by the learner has led to significant improvements in teaching efficiency as teachers have sought to engage their students' minds to create their own understandings. Students enjoy the independence, and teachers can focus on inspiring and encouraging them instead of goading and warning them to learn something because "it's important."

But the process takes time, and sometimes students use their time inefficiently. Then we feel tempted to resort to the conveyor belt approach to get some learning accomplished. But while students may appear to be wasting time, when they do make their own discoveries these are far more meaningful and valuable to them than what they recall from enduring one unit quickly following the last, with little attention to the values and principles they would enjoy and benefit from learning.

Yes, in some cases, the rare student quietly and on her own develops insights and constructs her schemas, sometimes even developing a passion for the field. That's what most of us who became teachers did—went through the rote units but man-

> "It matters when teachers see learning through the lens of the student grappling to construct beliefs and knowledge about whatever is the goal of the lesson. This is never linear, not always easy, requires learning and over learning, needs dollops of feedback, involves much deliberative practice, leads to lots of errors and mis-directions, requires both accommodating and assimilating prior knowledge and conceptions, and demands a sense of excitement and mission to know, understand, and make a difference." (Hattie 2008, 238)

aged to find some structure and meaning in them. We hope to inspire our students to do the same. But we cannot engender this effectively if the students do not grapple with the big concepts and instead temporarily store information and do not develop insights that alter their worldview. We want to reach both those rare students ripe to love our field as well as the students who feel less inspired.

Constructivism is a fine methodology, but we can improve on it. The teaching principles in this book take constructivism beyond the general idea that the students create knowledge to the more focused goal of developing students' critical thinking skills in the discipline. The goal is to compel students to process information, interrogate it, match it up to their current worldview, and revise it as needed, creating schemas that logically store information, insights, and the larger values that hold them together.

Thus this book does not suggest that students create simulated worlds, skits, poster projects, fictional diary entries, letters to the editor, and the like. These activities have their place in building empathy and in developing creative expression, especially at the middle and elementary school levels, but they cannot do the work of integrating concepts and information into a cohesive mental schema because it's too easy to select one isolated aspect of the problem and run with that, missing the opportunity for deeper enrichment. To accomplish the latter, students need to participate in cognitive analysis by sifting through plenty of information; developing, defending, and debating theories; detecting patterns; probing anomalies; and learning how to transfer concepts to new situations.

Some constructivist theorists suggest that teachers elicit students' prior knowledge about a topic before teaching a unit in order to get them thinking about it. However, it is not the student's (usually paltry) knowledge that needs to be brought to the forefront, but rather the student's way of understanding how the world works in regard to this topic, so that misconceptions can be considered in the light of how things really work. That's why it is so important for students to engage in genuine problem solving, to practice real critical thinking.

It is insufficient simply to ask students what they know right now and then try to fill in the blanks with what they should know. Rather, students need to grapple with a problem that forces them to face their misconceptions directly. As they try to explain anomalies, defend their ideas, assess the ideas of others, students finally reach a point where they alter their own worldview because they understand the topic more accurately.

In the process, students hone their critical thinking skills, learning how to suspend judgement, look for alternative ways of understanding, identify what else needs to be learned, and become less attached and more circumspect about their own assumptions. They also begin to mature in their ability to discuss problems with peers since they must listen carefully and offer tactful and genuine reflective observations of others' ideas in order to reach a valid consensus.

As students confront challenges that conflict with their own preconceptions, they may resort to rote memorization and simplistic thinking. When this occurs, it is up to the teacher to compel them to stretch and think more deeply so that they can

"Present students with experiences [challenges] that cause cognitive conflict in students' minds. Experiences . . . that can cause cognitive conflict are ones that get students to consider their erroneous (misconception) knowledge side-by-side with, or at the same time as, the correct concept or theory." (Lucariello and Naff 2009)

eventually place information into a valid schema. Doing so gives them a framework to which to attach the new information.

This process may have happened invisibly and intuitively for the teacher because his schemas were built up through encountering numerous examples (in college, graduate school, recreational reading) and his sheer and intense interest led him to see patterns and make connections. Typically, this takes years. But now we can give our students a leg up on this process and help them start building schemas and encountering threshold concepts early. Learning can become more efficient.

From a metacognitive perspective, experts and masters in a discipline are aware when they need further information and will stop to do some research to fill in missing gaps. But novices are not as adept at understanding their own learning process and thus waste time pursuing the wrong line of thought. They are far less efficient than experts. We can aid students by teaching them to pay attention to the steps they took to reach a fuller understanding of a threshold concept. And we can encourage them not to give up along the way, assuring them that they will eventually master these concepts, that their efforts are worthwhile.

Students almost invariably experience the confronting of a new threshold concept as a threat to their comfortable worldview, and they may mask their resistance behind a superficial understanding that they hope the teacher will accept. However, through grappling deeply with information and being compelled to explain it, they begin to feel some ambiguity about their preconceptions and become more willing to question them.

When courses are designed to accommodate how students learn best, teachers spend less time quizzing and testing and more time assessing students' thinking, pointing out to them when it is effective and when it is not. Teaching how to learn effectively in this discipline becomes part of the course.

Now that the teacher has decided where to focus and what to teach, she can decide how to teach so that students truly engage the topic and have a fair chance at identifying threshold concepts and engaging their misconceptions productively.

"Conceptual learning is holistic and is not transferred wholly so understanding is partial and fluid until the concept is fully engrained. The map can be actually wrong even when we consistently use the same words, phrases, signifiers. When [students] use the concept in discourse this is part of solidifying understanding." (Meyer and Land 2006)

5

How to Teach

Design Lessons That Compel Students to Confront Their Misconceptions

> Efforts to make threshold concepts "easier" by simplifying their initial expression
> and application may, in fact, set students onto a path of "ritualized" knowledge
> that actually creates a barrier that results in some students being prevented from
> crossing the "threshold" of a concept. (Meyer and Land 2006, xviii)

Once we have envisioned what needs to be taught, we can revise our lessons to put
the responsibility for learning on the student, because "she or he who does, learns."
Students must confront their misconceptions and replace them with accurate schemas
and also link them to related ones. Prioritizing this activity takes time and may require
a reduction in lectures and retrieval exercises to offer more opportunities for students
to grapple with intellectual challenges. Only information useful to students discovering the threshold concepts and associating them with relevant information is needed.

As the class is pared down to allow more time for students to learn how to think
in the discipline, the teacher's role will change from that of an information giver to
an advisor and Socratic questioner, pushing students to think beyond the box of their
preconceived notions. As students revise and enhance their schemas and worldview and
populate them with pertinent information, they will exhibit dramatic improvement in
their ability to retrieve information. This is because they can access a whole schema
of information, not "hunt and peck" for details. The schema is a network of content,
theory, and understandings woven together in a way that makes sense to the student.

The lesson design process should focus on getting students to discover the truth
themselves, crossing the "threshold" through observation and theorizing in a more
sophisticated version of their childhood learning method of "bumping into the
world" and either confirming or finding that they need to alter their worldview. The
lesson should start with a challenge or problem for students to solve, one that forces
them to confront their misconceptions.

Challenges can take the form of conducting experiments (like pushing a bowl-ing ball in a circle and speculating why it doesn't stay on the curve), analyzing why there are competing accounts of an event (such as the various explanations for why Truman dropped the first atomic bombs), or working out a thought problem (such as what the impact would be of a transcontinental railroad on the economy, society, politics, and ideas). It can also be as simple as asking students to inductively develop a theory about a grammar concept by studying examples and discussing their observations with their peers.

Figure 5.1 contains a lesson that has students teach themselves about compound and complex sentences.

The rule the students came up with in figure 5.1 is too general. Ask them to do the following:

- Put a box around each "sentence" in each example.
- Decide whether the sentences are the same.
- Decide what relationship, if any, exists between them.

The students in figure 5.2 are getting closer. Ask them if the comma joins or separates. Some of the students might know the term *clause* and use it. Make sure all of the students in the group can explain it.

You could now share with students the terms *compound sentence, complex sentence, independent clause,* and *subordinate clause* at this point, or wait for the whole-class

---

Inductive Grammar Lesson

In your group, examine and discuss the example sentences and formulate a rule to which they conform. All members of the group must be able to explain your reasoning. Each example sentence is grammatically correct and punctuated accurately.

A. In this set, all of the following sentences fit the rule.

- Sunny drove her car to the beach, but she didn't take her brother Gray.
- Gray sat in his room listening to music, although he would rather have gone to the beach with Sunny.
- Sunny ran across the soft, warm sand at the beach, and soon she saw waves perfect for surfing.

Write your rule here: *Two full sentences can be joined by a comma.*

Figure 5.1.

B. In this set, not all of the examples follow the rule. Examine the examples and revise your rule, if necessary. Be able to explain any examples that do not fit the rule. All members of the group must be able to explain your reasoning.

- Sunny knew that not every wave had potential, so she studied them carefully.

- She also scanned the sea for sharks, hoping not to see one.

- When she saw a wave she liked, Sunny hopped on her board and stood up.

- Sunny nimbly stepped off the board as soon as she got into the shallow surf.

Write your revised rule here: Sentences can be joined by a comma and a connector word, but one sentence is more important than the other.

Figure 5.2.

discussion. You could also mention *coordinating conjunction* and *subordinating conjunction* as well, but these terms are not that important.

What is important is that students:

1. Can routinely recognize and accurately create the pattern of compound and complex sentences.
2. Can determine the rule themselves instead of being told.
3. Can integrate this new understanding into their worldview of how sentences work.

The students in figure 5.3 understand the rule. To consolidate their learning, they need to process more examples and write a variety of correct subordinate clause sentences. This builds confidence in their rule. Students enjoy these short grammar lessons. They get to talk things out together, which they like, and they are creating, not passively being told—a big issue for most teens!

This lesson can easily be cloned for other grammar concepts. One could ask students to create their own lessons on specific grammar concepts. Then they could try out the lessons on their classmates, improve them, and thus build their own grammar "book." It's a complete inversion in the dynamic of teaching and learning (shall we call it "flipped"?), and students appreciate the chance to take on responsibility for work that both helps them and is fun to do.

C. Write one sentence that follows the rule and one that does not follow it but is still grammatically correct and punctuated accurately. All members of the group must be able to explain the difference, using the terms *independent clause* and *subordinate clause.*

Write your best version of the rule here: *A compound sentence contains an independent clause and a dependent clause. The independent clause contains the main idea, and the dependent clause adds more information to the independent clause. They must be separated by a comma and connected by a subordinating word or phrase.*

Write a sentence that follows the rule here: *Sunny got a lot of high-fives from onlookers even though her performance wasn't that impressive.*

Write a sentence that seems close but does not follow the rule here: *Sunny ran back into the water, hoping for an even longer run this time.*

Be ready to present your examples and able to explain the difference during our class discussion.

Figure 5.3.

The next example uses an online vocabulary program, Membean.com, which starts the learning of a new word by asking the student to infer its meaning from example usage (figure 5.4). Figure 5.5 is "memory hook" from Membean.

Finally, we have an example of an extended project from an advanced American Literature class that allows students to explore a social issue in depth. It starts with each student reading a different nonfiction book on such topics as water scarcity, consumerism, race relations, growing up gay, mental health policies, poverty, and political bias in the news. Since they choose the book themselves, students already have an interest in the topic; now they become the class expert on it. They read and summarize each chapter of their book, describing the rhetorical strategies (metaphors, statistics, testimonials, rhetorical questions, maps, and so on) that the author uses to convince his or her audience. They do the same thing for articles they find on the topic, which must include at least one that opposes the premise of their book.

Then they write a four-minute speech on what they most urgently want their classmates to understand about their topic. They also design an essay question on the topic. Each student receives a different essay question from a classmate, along with five to six excerpts from his or her book and articles so that the student can use that material to write an informed opinion essay. The student who designed the question scores that student's essay on it. This activity helps to prepare them for the "Synthesis Question" on the AP English Language exam (similar to AP History Document-Based Question essay).

As a *sagacious* or wise therapist, Anna Weld helped clients reach their own decisions rather than simply telling them how to solve their problems. Her famed insight attracted patients who needed her knowledgeable or *sagacious* advice, but she was careful to support rather than control their progress. Many were surprised when Dr. Weld decided to close her practice, but they knew that the *sagacious*, practical, and rational professional must have had good reasons to do so.

Q<small>uiz:</small> When is someone considered *sagacious*?

> a. When that person serves others kindly.

> b. When that person possesses great wisdom.

> c. When that person sees things that others cannot.

Definition

Figure 5.4.
Credit: Membean, used with permission

For their speeches, students must include several types of rhetorical strategies and stylish language, such as parallel structure, chiasmus, and alliteration. To that end, students can do some "finger exercises" during class, where the teacher puts a stylish sentence on the board and asks each student to write a new sentence in the same format, but applied to the content of their topic. Then students can read them aloud and analyze why they are effective. A sentence that is balanced, like an antimetabole (for example, Bill Clinton's comment that "People the world over have always been more impressed by the power of our example than by the example of our power"), seems to fully encapsulate the true and final word on the subject; the balance of the crisscross of "power" and "example" indicates a balanced thinker, one who understands the world in a thoughtful way.

Melody Flowing
The flowing melody singing forth from the mellifluous notes of the flute soothed us all.

Figure 5.5.
Credit: Membean, used with permission

The students carefully craft their speeches so that their rhetoric, too, showcases their ideas admirably. Then they present them on panels with other students who researched similar topics. After the whole panel has spoken, the audience asks questions.

Privately, for further practice in analyzing arguments, each audience member also sends the teacher an email identifying at least one logical fallacy committed by someone on that day's panel. The question-and-answer period is lively as students learn more about a controversial topic. The presentations get streamed live (and archived) so that the parent, faculty, and student community can watch and can email a question to pose "from the Internet audience."

This project is very popular, and incoming students look forward to it with excitement. It is especially rewarding to see students confidently articulating their beliefs and demonstrating deep knowledge. In addition, some of the students come back years later to say that they are now actively involved in solving the problem they presented on in the class.

The lesson format could easily be applied to any discipline. Once again, this is a project where students take ownership, seek mastery over the material, and share their findings with pride. They do the work, they do the learning, and they grow as thinkers and citizens.

No matter the assignment, the teacher should not front-load the learning process by giving students formulas, summaries, or simplified versions because doing so enables students to avoid thinking. It is the student's job to process pertinent information, but it is the teacher's job to provide clear and focused resources. There is no reason to send students out to wade through the often questionable information on the Internet when we can provide valid resources to them. Then students develop a theory about what is happening and why, while building a foundation of organized information to support it and that they can store as a vivid schema or analogy in their minds.

As practitioners, our knowledge of our discipline is well structured and firmly embedded in our minds, ready to recall. When we encounter a problem or question in our field, our minds immediately try out different schemas and analogies to find a fit. It's as though we superimpose a helpful map over the chaos, or have X-ray eyes that penetrate to the salient features, easily discerning the pieces, patterns, relationships, and anomalies.

To our students, however, our carefully designed challenges may seem like a pile of senseless and disassociated stuff, as though we have just dumped out the parts for an unidentified IKEA product and have not provided a picture and the assembly instructions. Yet, once the item is partially constructed, the pieces start to fit in more easily and the overall pattern or purpose becomes evident. That's what happens in natural learning. As the students process the problem, making comparisons and associations, they cannot help but begin to think, to organize the ideas, and to see a pattern emerge. With time, they become more comfortable with some initial ambiguity as they develop better strategies for problem solving through critical thinking.

Figure 5.6 represents the difference between the way a practitioner's understanding is organized and interconnected and the way the novice understanding is at first scattered and disorganized, unless steps are taken to cause the students to organize their thoughts into an analogy while they learn.

Teachers can help students by pointing out the metacognitive processes they follow as they learn, such as noting when inferences were made, asking students how they derived the inference, recognizing when students notice bias in a source or compare competing perspectives, and confirming the soundness of their logic. Eventually, the attention paid to how they process their ideas will lead them to notice the process of their own thinking as well, which opens a space for growth in critical thinking in general.

They also become more proficient at finding analogies that improve understanding and recall, more adept at organizing information and their own thoughts into a logical pattern. Of course, the more examples processed, the richer and more "thickly" the schema will be populated and mapped with facts, examples, traits, and connections. Students will employ their natural way of thinking and learning. The schema becomes even sturdier and richer when teachers give them borderline, extreme, or unusual examples to process. This strengthens, deepens, and multiplies connections within the schema and to other related schemas. This is learning.

To start the process of redesigning lessons, a teacher might begin with some questions: Which of my units have a clear connection to a core or threshold concept?

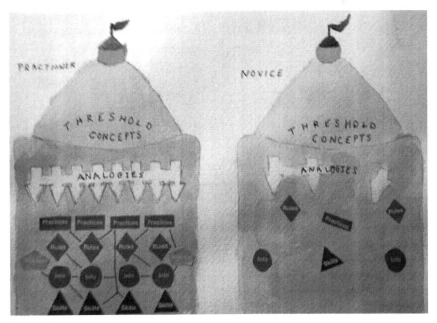

Figure 5.6.

How can I make this connection more explicit, and how can I rearrange my lesson so that students can discover the value or theory on their own? When I give them a challenge to work on, how will I handle questions to which I do not have an answer? How much information do I want to give them if I do? How can I identify other threshold concepts in my field? (See Appendix E for sample threshold concepts and skills from various courses.)

The examples and discussion above should make more clear how to design lessons that engage students' critical thinking. Before continuing on to the last step of course planning, how to assess student performance, we will consider one of the best methods of compelling students to think critically about a topic and to productively compare evidence to what they currently understand. The method is called modeling instruction. All who have tried it, whether in a single lesson, a whole unit, or an entire course, praise its ability to engage students fully, to hone their ideas through debate with their peers, to help them visualize the topic or problem in a spatial way that leads to better retention, and to develop analogies that can organize information in the students' minds.

THE MODELING INSTRUCTION METHOD

There are many ways to implement threshold concepts where students learn independently, make theories, and develop analogies to organize their learning. However, one method stands out for its ability to compel students to face their misconceptions, visualize what is happening, and develop valid theories. It is called modeling instruction.

Recall that modeling instruction, first pioneered by physics teachers and now widely used in that discipline with an average of double the retention rate of standard teaching, is a method that has students run experiments, draw diagrams of what happens, gather and analyze data, and speculate on a theory that explains their findings. The same process can be used in other disciplines, with changes to accommodate the kind of information to be analyzed.

Students, in small groups (three members is ideal since no one can "hide"), take responsibility for their approach and learning, they diagram the theory that they produce, and they present their findings to the class. Small-group work requires them to explain and defend an idea, and as a bonus it satisfies students' desire to talk things out with their peers.

Modeling instruction is a teaching practice that involves small groups of students constructing core concepts and rules with only minimal teacher guidance. The students in their groups process readings, artifacts, and other data sources (including results from experiments), reaching a consensus on their understanding through dialogue, drawing, and presentation of their results.

Modeling instruction looks a bit like inquiry or student-centered leaning, but it takes these concepts to a new plateau of learning efficiency, having been designed according to the latest insights from cognitive science into how the brain learns. Physics teachers have capitalized on the effectiveness of modeling instruction for over ten years, but it has not been used much outside of the sciences until recently.

Modeling instruction began when a college physics teacher, Malcolm Wells, discovered that even when using inquiry-based teaching methods, students generally did not exceed a 40 percent retention rate. He realized that no matter how much the teacher asserted the rules of physics, the students systematically misunderstood them and continued to apply their own, pre-Newtonian concepts to the experiments and homework problems. However, physics teachers who used modeling instruction, even when fairly new to the method, achieved retention rates of 60 to 80 percent.

This was measured using the "Force Concept Inventory," a carefully designed multiple-choice test developed by Malcolm Wells, David Hestenes, and Gregg Swackhamer where the distractor choices reveal students' specific incorrect physics concepts. It is now a standard test of student retention in physics. Modeling instruction succeeds because students in modeling classes develop their own visual representations of theories, processes, and forces, which enhances their understanding of the material presented.

In a mechanical physics course that uses modeling, students conduct the usual lab experiments but set out on their path of learning without formulas or textbook problems to solve. Instead, they diagram what is physically happening and explain their theories to each other. They extract their theory from the data and then try it out on new problems, predicting what their results will be. In this fashion, their understanding of the physicality of the problems evolves before they encounter the associated formulas.

This process causes them to confront their own embedded, preconceived notions. For example, in a unit on force concepts, students typically make predictions loosely based on the Aristotelian concept of impetus (that an object only moves if pushed). Despite numerous experiments and even despite knowing the correct formula, their understanding of the nature of force exists as a metaphor that contradicts the Newtonian physics their experiments are proving.

A well-designed unit in modeling instructions generates a conceptual conflict for the students and causes them to confront their incorrect preconceived notions and correct them through dialogue with their peers. The moment of engaging in the conflict causes a kind of cognitive dissonance, which the student will want to avoid. But it must come out in the dialogue with her peers so that she can examine it more closely. As the group reaches consensus on a diagram that represents what really happens, the students' internal model of the physical world also changes to represent reality.

Now, with better understanding, students need only study the eight core diagrams they produce over the year that make up mechanical physics. Most other physics courses likewise rest on a small handful of core models, so instead of studying formulas to prepare for exams, students can simply study how their diagrams work and what kinds of problems they apply to. Now the formulas are also easier to memorize and recall because they can be rederived from the diagrams and graphs that make physical sense to the student. The same applies in math, chemistry, and biology classes where there exist a finite number of core principles (actually, threshold concepts) that use modeling instruction.

MODELING INSTRUCTION IN HUMANITIES AND OTHER CLASSES

In humanities classes (and literature, psychology, environmental science, and so on), retention and deep understanding also need to be addressed. Students too often cram for tests and afterward forget much of the material. Thus key skills and concepts have to be retaught year after year. Students also often fail to see the forest for the trees, memorizing rules, dates, and names without the flexibility to apply core concepts and patterns to different contexts. As in the physical sciences, students need to visualize a correct internal image of, for example, how an essay should be structured or how historical forces operate, as their teachers and experts in the field do automatically.

However, physics instruction differs profoundly from instruction in humanities and other nonscience classes in that physics is an established system of rules and formulas that are essentially agreed upon across the discipline. No such hard-and-fast rules exist in history, environmental science, psychology, or English, except for the most basic rules and concepts. Instead, there may be a loose consensus among history practitioners about what happened in a given time and place, but not necessarily about why it did. In English there is consensus on things like rules of grammar and citation, but there is a lot of latitude on textual interpretation, choice of materials, and pedagogical methods.

Ultimately, whereas physics modelers have established a fixed and finite canon and methodology, humanities and other nonscience classes have flexible canons and varying teaching methods. Does this mean that modeling cannot work in these disciplines? No. The advantages of modeling still obtain, and the process is nearly identical. The only difference will be in the materials students study and the models they produce. Whereas physics models will be visibly similar for a given topic, models from other types of disciplines will be more rich and diverse, even within a single classroom. The value still lies in the actual creation of the models, in the dialogue that produces them, and in the discussion afterward that exposes and corrects inaccurate understandings.

The modeling process pushes students to develop metaphors and create connections, often cross-referencing their knowledge from other disciplines. For example, in developing a model on cultural diffusion through trade, a group might draw an image of the semipermeable barrier of a living cell to represent the combination of free flow and restriction in a particular trade system. The process of discussing and creating these metaphors and connections, along with the visual diagramming, makes abstract concepts meaningful and memorable so that students retain their understandings and can apply them to similar situations.

The focus of the model is on broad concepts—for example, theoretical frameworks, forces, and themes, that is, the why more than the who, what, where, or when. The latter are still processed by the student, but in modeling this information serves as source material (like lab data) from which to extract underlying processes, forces, or theories. A student who understands, for example, the way the transcontinental railroad in the United States acted as a force of change, of technology overcoming nature, and of transportation as a spur to migration or as a means of exclusion can see how that same pattern of consequences occurs with other new technologies, such as the telephone, television, superhighway, or Internet.

Students consider aspects that experts consider: defining and refining their terms, examining the relevance and credibility of sources, and making use of methods and metaphors from other disciplines, creating strong links among their domains of knowledge as well as solidifying their understanding of the topic under study. Class discussions become seminars of peers in which all are engaged.

In one simple exercise, English teachers can ferret out students' misconceptions about how an essay should be organized. Asked to diagram the shape and connections in a standard essay, students often develop a visual model of the essay that departs significantly from what their teacher expects, yet this internal map is the foundation from which their students produce their essays. Unlike their teachers, students seldom visualize the network of connections between the sections of an essay (the link between the thesis and topic sentences, the sentence-to-sentence links that provide cohesion in body paragraphs, etc.).

Time spent in conferencing is wasted as the teacher unknowingly battles an unseen and inaccurate schematic that is driving their students' most important decisions about writing, just as novice physics students unconsciously harbor Aristotelian misconceptions about force. When student groups share their models of essay structure and discuss the merit of each, the class creates a common vocabulary and new vision of what is expected. Gaining a class consensus on a correct structure for an essay, settling on one version that all can copy and keep in their notes, makes instruction and conferencing more efficient as the teacher can ask students to point out where their essay conforms to or diverts from the ideal essay structure the class created.

Modeling instruction can be implemented into the curriculum incrementally. First, teachers identify a core concept, one that can be expressed visually. Then, they select readings and other materials that present focused, concrete, and vivid examples of the concept, where the structures are easily laid bare by the students. Several sources with the same forces at play reinforce core ideas and increase students' confidence. The goal is to cause students to invent their own problem-solving procedures by first extracting and confirming a visual diagram, then applying that pattern when they write.

In designing new modeling instruction units, teachers ask themselves questions like the following:

- What source materials contain bold outlines?
- What examples represent the full range and scope of the concept?
- What are the core structures and concepts?
- What can we measure?

- What can we display visually?
- What forces act, and upon what?
- What patterns, cycles, and connections exist?

Expert teachers perceive their discipline visually, knowing what connects to what and understanding the hierarchy of ideas and information, but their students do not. They know the big picture as well as the small. By diagramming and using these models themselves, students begin to fit the small items into the bigger picture. They begin to understand the nature of the life cycle of civilizations, the structures of different genres of writing, the conflict between conservation efforts and economics, the pressures placed on historical and contemporary leaders.

In other words, they begin to see the discipline as a practitioner does. They also improve their critical thinking in the discipline. Even starting with a small modeling instruction unit will result in better understanding and retention.

HOW MODELING INSTRUCTION WORKS

The central activity of modeling instruction is done in small groups of students (ideally, three) using two-by-three-foot whiteboards to prepare a diagram of a concept. The whiteboards have multiple functions: they provide a medium for communication, establish the scope of the problem, and record insights. Whiteboards are preferred over large sheets of paper or computers because they can easily be erased and revised throughout the thinking process.

Whiteboards also provide a convenient size for small-group work; three students can easily access and see the board, and all of them can have something to say in what gets diagrammed. The whiteboard is not considered finished until the whole group agrees that what is on the board represents their united conception of the theory or idea being modeled (though dissenting views can be included). Group dynamics shift and grow as the students use the markers and the eraser in their search for consensus.

Creating a meaningful diagram might lead to developing a schema or useful analogy that will make the theory easier to understand and remember. Recall that cognitive scientists say that analogy lies at the core of thinking. Analogies and metaphors help frame concepts because one can picture them and map the traits of the concept onto the corresponding traits of an analogy, providing a meaningful framework for storing information and examples.

The process begins with data, information, or evidence, such as reading a novel or memoir, reviewing a historical account, examining statistics, or watching a film. The purpose is to inform students about the topic. Material should be clear and focused, with few distractions, so that students can focus on the important aspects of the topic. Choosing materials for modeling instruction is an art in itself, and getting a good range of different opinions makes the sources even more interesting to students. Spending the time to develop a good source packet is time well spent.

After reading and discussing each resource, students go through a sifting process, deciding what aspect of the materials they want to explain. Sometimes the teacher gives the student groups a specific topic, either a variety so that each group has a different angle from which to view the material or the same topic for all. As the students sift through their ideas, they decide what evidence they want to include.

Next they begin to diagram how the different entities interact with each other. For example, in a unit on the relations between Indians and the Puritans, students might note that there is a two-way arrangement of trade, disease, cooperation, and also resentment. As students draw, they revise and perfect their theory, reaching a consensus through discussion and defending their own ideas.

All students need to participate because each of them must be able to explain their reasoning behind their work. Inconsistencies are revealed, requiring revisions to the diagram but also to the students' initial ideas. Now students revise their diagram to reflect their growing theoretical framework, the "forest" that they have extracted from the "trees" of the materials read and presented by the teacher.

The drawing represents the "shape" of their idea. In physics, this entails drawing graphs and lines representing the forces they observed in their experiments and patterns they find in data collected and tabulated. In the humanities, students might diagram the forces acting on a character or historical figure or depict a pattern seen in events, consequences, or literary structures. The best diagrams are clean, with simple, clear shapes and arrows representing large forces, relationships, and patterns. They are representations that students can manipulate, mentally or actually, to depict different situations or to be applied to different situations. The goal is not to create a work of art or cartoon but to create a tool for discussion.

During this time, the teacher moves from group to group, listening carefully to what the students say and asking strategic, clarifying questions to help them see things differently if needed. This supervision can be described as a kind of "Socratic hovering," in which the teacher listens in on each group's deliberations but does not interfere with the students' process other than to ask a few questions as they work. Even if a group gets it wrong, the teacher does not intervene. Other students in the class may point out the problem later during the whole-class "board meeting," or they may not. It takes a lot of courage to let the moment slip by to be addressed another day, but by not intervening, the teacher gives the students the strong message that their learning is up to them.

The teacher might, very occasionally, ask questions to help a student clarify the sometimes-nebulous image in his or her mind, but it is better to err on the side of not interfering, unless a group is completely off-target. This kind of teaching requires mastery over the content as well as the typical conceptual errors that students tend to make, a teaching skill that improves over time. In physics, only after the class has adequately articulated a correct theory will the teacher give them the formulas that usually get presented at the beginning of a physics unit under traditional teaching. The same should occur in other courses so that the students themselves come up with a variety of valid theories that can be further discussed, debated, and clarified.

After the boards are complete, students gather in a circle and place their whiteboard at their feet so that all can see every board in preparation for the presentations. Placing boards in this pattern facilitates efficient discussion as students can easily compare results, generating questions on why a particular element was included or excluded. The board diagrams serve as a springboard for a rich, full-class, student-led conversation.

The diagrams themselves will probably not be meaningful to outsiders, as it is the rationale behind the design that matters and that produces the most provocative insights. Therefore, students explain how the elements of their diagram represent the theory their group has developed. Some groups will have well-developed theories and diagrams, while others will be less encompassing and may even contain errors of analysis and judgment.

The group discussion exposes these inconsistencies, not to find fault but to account for differences and missing or incongruent elements. As students gain confidence, they learn to separate themselves from their work, allowing for greater insights. With modeling instruction, a lot of learning occurs as the class listens to the small groups and notes differences among the theories and diagrams.

Students run these discussions, with only occasional interjections by the teacher to reflect questions back to the class or to ask another student to rephrase or interpret what has just been said, bringing quiet students back into the conversation. Ultimately, the teacher cannot force students to discover; this process occurs on its own and often the students reach insights that the teacher would not have anticipated. As students ask each other questions, they improve their skills in negotiating group dynamics, develop higher-order thinking skills, and master the material.

Ideally, student groups work independently, without any scaffolding from the teacher. Because groups are asked to agree on their theory, and each student is held accountable to be able to explain it fully, the students get valuable practice in articulating, defending, and revising their ideas—that is, in critical thinking. They will also each be forced to confront their misconceptions and to decide how to revise them to fit reality. Because they cannot hide in a group of three students or so, they are forced to think, and this leads them, eventually, to reconnect with their innate desire to learn. The process helps stimulate students to become the learners they are inclined to be.

WHY MODELING INSTRUCTION WORKS

A few key concepts from cognitive science help to explain why modeling is so effective. It has to do with the fact that spatial-visual knowledge is stored in a different brain area than language is. Long-term memory and spatial-visual knowledge reside at the core of the brain, primarily in the hippocampus. This area, one of the oldest parts of the brain, adequately handled the spatial needs of the prelanguage human. It stored (as it continues to do) memories, visual maps, motor skills, and spatial navigation. The language areas (spoken, verbal, written, symbolic), which came later in human development, exist in several centers of the brain, sometimes called the conceptual reasoning regions.

Another cognitive function transfers information across the boundary between the spatial-visual and language brain areas. As this boundary is crossed, the learner creates an internal schematic, manipulates it mentally, and then associates language with that schematic. When cross-boundary transfer does not occur, verbal or symbol information comes in and new words or symbols come out, without achieving deep understanding.

Modeling's use of multiple representations (diagrams, graphs, words, equations, discussion, debate) forces the student to cross this language/spatial-visual interface again and again. When students diagram the relationships between ideas, they are operating at the spatial reasoning level. As they develop a working model, the language perception of the spatial map is coordinated to it through dialogue with peers and teacher.

As discussed earlier, cognitive scientists agree that in infants, the mind works primarily on a level of spatial representations (essentially, geometric shapes, location, orientation, and patterns) and that language is actually founded upon spatial reasoning. This can be corroborated by noticing how many spatial metaphors undergird our language.

For example, we often use the metaphor of life as a "road" that can be "traveled," where decisions are thought of as which "path" to take. Furthermore, we associate values with directional adverbs, such as *above* and *close*, which imply, respectively, *better* and *intimate*. It is insufficient, however, for the teacher simply to provide his or her own metaphoric or spatial map of the information being taught. Students must create their own conceptual frameworks, working at the level of spatial representation (that is, below the level of language).

In this way, they place their theoretical knowledge at the very core of the mind in visual-spatial imagery, where it becomes embedded in their memory and understanding of the way the world works. Because they devise and employ their own metaphors, the brain is fully engaged and learning is loaded into long-term memory. Because these visual-spatial memories now contribute to the students' worldview, they can be deployed in new situations, increasing students' proficiency at general problem solving as well.

Empirical studies of successful instruction methods also demonstrate the power of modeling instruction. In 2001, Robert Marzano identified nine effective teaching strategies. Modeling instruction uses all nine of them (Marzano, Pickering, and Pollock 2001). In addition, modeling engages six of Howard Gardner's (2006) eight intelligences. More recently, of the top ten evidence-based teaching methods analyzed by John Hattie (2008) in his survey of over eight hundred teaching methods, modeling instructions employs all ten (see figure 5.7).

Beyond matching these top indicators, modeling instruction engages students in genuine critical thinking, because critical thinking is central to conducting research

Marzano's 9 Effective Teaching Strategies	Modeling Instruction	Gardner's 8 Intelligences	Modeling Instruction	Hattie's Top 10 Teaching Methods	Modeling Instruction
Identifying similarities and differences	√	Linguistic	√	Be clear about what students should learn	√
Reinforcing effort and providing recognition	√	Logical-mathematical	√	Tell student what they need to know and do	√
Homework and practice	√	Spatial	√	Question students to check understanding	√
Nonlinguistic representation	√	Kinesthetic	√	Have students summarize information in a graph	√
Cooperative learning	√	Interpersonal	√	Give students practice spaced over time	√
Setting objectives and providing feedback	√	Intrapersonal (knowledge of self)	√	Provide students with feedback so they can revise	√
Generating and testing hypotheses	√	Musical		Have students work together in productive ways	√
Cues, questions, [and advance organizers]	√	Naturalist		Teach students strategies as well as content	√
				Nurture metacognition	√

Figure 5.7.

and creating theories, as modeling instruction requires students to do. In addition, it compels students to face their own misconceptions and to revise their faulty logic and worldview with a more accurate understanding of reality.

Modeling instruction holds tremendous promise for better critical thinking and retention. It offers a way for teachers to become more efficient at getting students to retain and truly understand material and to be adept and confident in applying it to new scenarios. By shifting the focus away from piling on more and more information to understanding and deploying core concepts, modeling instruction empowers students to become problem solvers, a skill that will be crucial to their success in our complex, troubled world.

To sum up, the small groups working on their challenges and problems should follow this four-step modeling instruction process:

1. Students process information in the form of materials provided by the teacher that engage a common conceptual challenge. The teacher knows from experience that this challenge often roots out misconceptions that students might hold. For clarity, she chooses materials that get straight to the point and have few distracting aspects. She provides a range of types of sources (film, text, maps, memoirs, statistics, daily record-keeping information, and so on). She also makes sure to include different points of view and opinions on the topic so that the students are compelled to compare them and decide which convince them the most.

2. Students discuss the materials and begin to consider various theories to explain what they have processed. Each student should advance and try to defend his

ideas against the ideas of the others in his group so it is important that each idea be put forth and defended.

3. Next, student groups develop visual/diagrammatic models that convey their understanding of the joint theory of what they learned. They diagram on erasable whiteboards. They can easily change, revise, and even start over on their drawings as their theory evolves. The images may include a few words to clarify elements of the model, but on the whole, the groups should represent the dynamics of their theory using abstract shapes and arrows. They might, for instance, make one square larger than another square to indicate more power or control, or use arrows to show the direction of that control.

4. Finally, student groups present their findings to the whole class in a "board meeting," explaining and defending their theory. Again, the teacher watches and listens, allowing the students to process the differences in the various theories as represented abstractly on the boards. Some students will have culminated their ideas in an analogy that vividly conveys their theory. Others may not reach that goal, but by viewing the other boards these students begin to realize how they can make an analogy for their theory. They will also correct their theory when other students convince them it is not complete.

Figure 5.8.

Figure 5.9.   Sometimes the diagrams reveal confusion.

Figure 5.10.   But other diagrams demonstrate deep understanding...

Figure 5.11. And pride of accomplishment!

After this process, students should test their theories and hypotheses by investigating whether or not their models successfully predict outcomes using other data.

In the modeling instruction mode of teaching, instead of explaining, lecturing, repeating, simplifying, and scaffolding, the teacher serves as a resource to students' deliberations, floating from group to group, answering questions or clarifying the source materials. The teacher must resist asking loaded questions or in other ways pushing the groups to a specific insight. Instead, he might ask a group why a certain part of the diagram looks confusing, or whether they have considered a given aspect of the source materials, but for the most part, students must be free to make mistakes so they get valuable practice in trying to defend their ideas.

In the diagram in figure 5.12, students have represented the social and economic effect of travel and trade along the silk road as a series of threads that get woven together as they interact. Their theory is that when traders from different cultures enter the market (as represented as the box in the center), they talk, share information, and slowly begin to adopt each other's ideas and values, changing all of the involved parties, making links between them, and creating a strong bond, as represented by the thick woven strand coming out of the right of the market box.

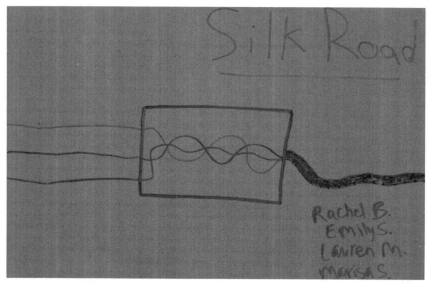

Figure 5.12.

Their version of the threshold concept was that "Cultures are enriched through trade and the social interaction that comes with trade." This group tried several different analogies before they struck on this one. One student would start a diagram, and the other students would detect a problem with it. So they erased and started over, about five times. The final drawing may be crude, but the theory is brilliant. The students who produced this diagram will long remember the lesson they taught themselves.

It is important to recall here that while students need analogies, metaphors, and schemas to best organize information, they should develop them themselves through grappling with the data, not by being told.

For further reading, see Appendix F, "Sample Student Challenges."

Having discussed how students learn (by analogy), how to tap into students' natural curiosity and enjoyment of thinking (presenting challenges that are neither too difficult nor too easy), and how to identify the core threshold concepts that make our disciplines exciting and worthy of study and addressed the first three course planning steps (where to focus, what to teach, and how to teach), we are now ready to address the last step of course planning, how to assess.

6

How to Assess

Design Ways to Gauge Students' Critical Thinking

To extend the analogy of the car mechanic used in the introduction, once an attempt has been made to fix the problem (the car stalling; our students not thinking), we need a way to look under the hood again to check whether the "engine" is now working properly. We want to "read" how our students think about what they know to determine if their thinking process is becoming more correct.

We may need to change our assessment procedures if we want to detect the thought processes that have led to what they say and write. We might also want to establish a baseline of the stage of their critical thinking skills about a given topic through preassessment at the beginning of the course or unit. Then we can compare pre- and postlearning assessments of the same skills to determine if and how much advancement has been achieved and what kind of remedial work they still need.

Again, we are not as interested in measuring retention of information as we are in measuring how students think. Nevertheless, having done some pretests at the beginning of the course, we could measure retention in order to assess whether we are getting results as good as the physics modeling instruction classes that achieved nearly double the retention rates. At the same time, though, we must create new assessments, as well as our manner of evaluating them, to assess our students' critical thinking skills. We have to learn how to read our students' minds, and we can.

Our assessments of the thinking process will be specific to our discipline: the ways of going about being a scientist, a historian, a mathematician, a literature expert, and so on. What habitual traits, beliefs, understandings, and thought processes make a scientist, a historian? How much have our students progressed toward mastering particular traits along the path of becoming a practitioner of our field? Have they acquired the basic skills and do they perform them automatically, without resorting to instructions? Have they begun to develop a more focused understanding of the next level of the practitioner? Are they still resisting the threshold concepts, or are there glimmers that these ideas are at least becoming familiar, if not ingrained in their worldview?

Because thinking goes on inside the brain, it takes skill and inference to "read" students' minds and assess not what they know but how they think. Teachers who listen carefully to how students frame their thoughts, express themselves, and answer questions can infer the kind of thinking that led to their statements.

How might we assess a group's whiteboard diagram? By analyzing the diagram, by listening to the students' logic about what it means, and by assessing the significance and fit of their theory.

In Figure 6.1, three students created a strong metaphor to express their theory about an important theme in *The Great Gatsby*. In the image, an elegant woman stands in front of a wall of houses with a bag of money sitting unattended on the ground nearby. Behind the wall, we see a sad man, a broken heart, and two puzzle pieces that don't fit together. The students wrote a sentence to explain their diagram: "Fitzgerald believes that society, in an attempt to create the American Dream, merely created a facade of frivolity, lavishness, and happiness, behind which they hide their inadequacies and sorrow." Their wall is the facade, and its impenetrability indicates that no reconciliation will occur. The diagram is thoughtful, evocative, and elegant—an image that all of the other students comprehended easily.

Figure 6.1.

As students and the teacher asked the group questions about the details of the diagram and theory, it became evident that these students had a firm grasp on the hopeless poverty of the American Dream, which lures people into chasing it but does not reward them with the happiness they expect. Each of the students in the group had something specific to explain about the symbols in their diagram. For example, one student explained that the puzzle pieces represented the many forged but tragically incomplete relationships (Tom and Daisy, Nick and Jordan, Myrtle and George, Myrtle and Tom).

Clearly, the group had worked together well, fueled each other's ideas, and produced a clear, powerful image and theory. They already had the thesis statement for their essay on the novel. A less sophisticated idea and diagram or a group that cannot fully explain their reasoning would represent a less successful example of critical thinking about the novel.

Next are two more assessment scenarios to consider. One is an example of assessing critical thinking skills in a class discussion of a text, and the other is an example of assessing critical thinking skills in a written essay.

ASSESSING CRITICAL THINKING
SKILLS IN A CLASS DISCUSSION

In this example, the class uses the Harkness method of discussion, in which students discuss topics of their choice as a class, not raising hands or interrupting each other but allowing others to jump in when the previous speaker stops. The teacher does not participate but rather creates a seating chart and takes notes on what each student says. Students can be graded on their contribution for the day. With practice and a crude form of shorthand, note taking gets more efficient over time.

In addition, the teacher can add observations about what kind of thought process the student used in order to make his comment. One might, for example, write "inference," or "probing question," or "claim, no warrant" next to a student's comment. As they discuss, the students know to allow someone to add on to a thread of conversation before letting another student change the topic. They can revisit topics again and ask the quiet students to contribute their thoughts. It's their show, but they know that the teacher listens for comments that do the following:

- Make inferences from the text and support them with logic
- Respect the ideas of others by examining them fairly
- Clarify, expand upon, or synthesize the ideas of others
- Explain the implications of an event or of a line of thinking
- Compare analogous situations and transfer insights between them
- Demonstrate confidence in one's reasoning
- Consider the author's purpose

Here's an excerpt from a class discussion of *The Great Gatsby*:

> Student A: Daisy cries when she sees Gatsby's shirts because she realizes what she has
> missed out on in life.

First, note that the student has mentioned a significant detail. Not everyone would
react to a pile of pretty shirts as Daisy does. Secondly, the student's statement is a
claim, though it is not supported by logic. It happens to be a valid claim, but one
could just as easily conclude that Daisy cries because she considers the shirts a waste
of money or that she fears that this kind of consumption habit threatens the environment. The student's thought is incomplete because it is unsubstantiated. One would
write "unsupported claim" in the notes.

> Student B: She cries because she realizes that Gatsby is a true romantic.

Student B has also made another unsubstantiated claim, but this claim is slightly
more focused and represents a more interesting interpretation than Student A's
comment. This student, too, has inferred that Daisy would have loved to have had
a romantic life with Gatsby. She bases her inference on Daisy's reaction and her insights about Gatsby, who is a hopeless romantic. Her comment is closer to the mark.

At this point, the teacher could ask the other students to name what both students
have done ("made an inference") and ask another student to explain how to support
these inferences with logic. Keep these interruptions to a minimum, but it is an opportunity for them to get familiar with the metacognition of critical thinking.

> Student C: I think Daisy cries because she realizes that a life with Gatsby would have
> been more romantic than the one she has with Tom, who would never buy such gor-
> geous shirts. She has come face-to-face with what is wrong with her marriage: it lacks
> romance.

This student has provided logical reasoning explaining the inference that Daisy cries
for her loss. The teacher would write "logical" next to her comment in the discussion notes.

> Student D: Why doesn't Daisy just leave Tom? He has affairs, and she doesn't love
> him—she loves Gatsby.

This student has raised an important implication, or potential consequence of the
insight the shirts give to Daisy. Not only does the student logically ask about the
consequences of discovering her need for romance, she also seems to have inferred
that Daisy probably will not leave Tom for Gatsby.

> Student E: Gatsby and Tom are two completely different people. Unlike Gatsby, Tom
> doesn't have any romantic illusions. He makes money, and he spends it. He does not

pine over girls he did not marry. Whereas Tom seems fully (if boringly) integrated in his world, Gatsby seems to float above it, staring longingly at a green dock light and fantasizing about a life he cannot have. He's just a dreamer.

This student has applied the idea of romanticism to make a comparison between Tom and Gatsby. This takes the class closer to considering what the author wants the reader to understand about the pursuit of wealth in America.

During the students' discussion, it is best simply to listen, stopping, if at all, only to ask students to identify the kinds of critical thinking they have heard so far. What inferences were made? Who provided reasoning for inferences? Who asked questions that opened up new lines of thinking? What comparisons helped others reach a deeper understanding? Who was able to synthesize different threads of thought? Listening carefully and taking notes on each student's contribution hones the teacher's ability to make informed assessments of the students' critical thinking skills.

What the teacher should not do is intervene in the students' deliberations by supplying the missing reasoning herself, or ask leading questions that prod students to a particular insight. As frustrating as it might be to stay quiet when students come very close to—and then drift away from—an important insight, the students themselves must make these discoveries, and they themselves must do the work to improve their own critical thinking skills.

The teacher's role is to help students recognize the moves they make, only occasionally commenting on the metacognitive aspects of the discussion. It is far more important that students hone their critical thinking skills than it is for them to reach a particular point of understanding in a particular class period. And if we do intervene, we will have taught them simply to wait until we provide "the answer." You can always start the conversation again a day later and ask them to push their interpretations further.

ASSESSING CRITICAL THINKING SKILLS IN WRITTEN RESPONSES

Assessing essay responses is an art that teachers practice quite a lot. This example demonstrates how asking the right questions sets students up for greater success.

Here is a history essay question:

What was the significance of the Battle of Antietam?

And a student essay response:

Even though the three-day Battle of Antietam was a draw, it was a significant event in the Civil War. In one day of September 1862, more than 22,000 soldiers died, making it the bloodiest day in American military history. General Robert E. Lee, after a few successful battles with the Union Army, marched boldly into Maryland, Union territory, in order to threaten Washington, DC. But a union soldier found a copy of his field orders (wrapped around three cigars) and notified Union General George McClellan, who had been sitting tight, fearing (incorrectly) that he was outnumbered. His army actually outnumbered Lee's by two to one. With the information about Lee's plans, McClellan, who was notorious for delaying too long before entering a battle, uncharacteristically took the initiative and for a time pushed back the Confederate forces. However, he failed to press for a decisive victory, allowing Lee to regroup and to set up his artillery. Then McClellan failed to send orders to his troops, and each commander had to decide what to do on his own; one unit never joined the battle at all. Eventually both sides lost so many men that the two generals agreed to a truce. Lee retreated. Both generals were criticized by the press for their performance. The battle is significant in that no land was gained or lost on either side, though the human cost was deplorable. In addition, the fact that Lee retreated back to the South improved President Lincoln's status in the eyes of the populace and led him to issue the Emancipation Proclamation.

This student clearly remembers a lot of information about the battle. Whether it came from lectures, reading, or research, he definitely knows what happened. But the question asks, what is significant about the Battle of Antietam. Did he answer it? Note that in the last two sentences, the student writes, "The battle is significant in that . . ." He remembers the goal and he fulfills it. But is this a strong essay? The student had to go into storytelling mode in order to fit significant events into his narrative.

A more analytical response would not move through the material consecutively but rather move from one significant factor to the next. The answer definitely demonstrates the student's familiarity with the battle and the generals, and it mentions the deplorable loss of life and the fact that Lee was unable to conquer Union territory, which led Lincoln to announce the Emancipation Proclamation. However, in the context of this essay, these are simply facts, basically a matter of information recall.

But we can hardly fault the student. He has responded adequately to the prompt and probably deserves an A. However, if it is critical thinking skills we want to measure, both the question and the answer fail the task. The prompt did not elicit critical thinking skills, so the student is able to get away with information recall. We need to design questions that elicit the kind of thinking we seek.

Here's a better question:

> In what way(s) did the Battle of Antietam represent a turning point in the American Civil War?

This question concerns the exact same topic as the previous question, but we can assess it differently—for evidence of understanding the threshold concept "The outcome of a single battle can influence the outcome of the war because of the psychological effect it has on both sides."

Note that if the essay above were written in reply to the second question, which asks how the battle represents a turning point, it does not suffice. To view the battle as a potential turning point requires the student to put the battle into the context of the larger war, to consider the psychological impact of the battle on both sides, and possibly to demonstrate an appreciation of Lincoln's strategy. The following would be a more than adequate response to the second question, and an absolutely stellar (though unlikely) response to the first:

> The three-day Battle of Antietam represented a turning point in three important ways: there were serious consequences for both generals, the outcome affected the psychological viewpoint of both the Union and the Confederacy, and the result of the battle influenced decisions at the national, and even international, level.
>
> It was a gruesome battle, with over 22,000 soldiers killed on one day. Although neither side technically won or lost, both generals experienced a personal negative turning point because of it. Gen. Robert E. Lee initiated the battle with the momentum of having recently won three important battles over the Union Army. He boldly decided to engage them on their own territory, in Maryland. But despite his brilliant military strategy on the field, he ultimately retreated in shame, losing credibility in the South. In a different way and for different reasons, General George McClellan also experienced a tragic turn. His flaw of avoiding risk through delay once again cost the Union the chance to win definitively. Even though he acted promptly in the first engagement (after getting a copy of Lee's battle plans), he afterward failed to give his commanding officers any orders at all, leaving them to devise their own plans and to somehow coordinate their moves with other units. One unit did not engage at all. So despite outnumbering Lee's forces, McClellan's army could not accomplish the victory that seemed easy to obtain. McClellan's turning point culminated with a fed-up Lincoln dismissing him for his negligence.
>
> On the sectional level, the Battle of Antietam represented a psychological turning point for both sides. Up until this battle, the Confederacy had strong hopes of winning the war. But Lee's retreat indicated that the Union Army had an equal chance. The Union, on the other hand, had felt less certain about the possibility of winning, and the populace felt increasingly doubtful about Lincoln's leadership as president. This was a problem since the election was coming up. Even though the battle was not decisive, the fact of Robert E. Lee's retreat encouraged Northerners and demonstrated that Lincoln's grand strategy was working: the Union Army could indeed prevail.
>
> At the national level, the outcome was also positive, for with this new credibility, Lincoln felt confident in publishing his draft of the Emancipation Proclamation, a move that ultimately led to the abolishment of slavery. Finally, at the international level, the Union's success in repulsing Lee gave pause to Britain and France, who were about to offer financial support to the Confederacy since they wanted to keep the South's cotton flowing to their mills. When they realized that the South might lose the war, they decided to wait and see. Not getting their funding was more bad news for the Confederacy. Battles are not just violent contests between armies. They can have wide-reaching psychological and strategic consequences that alter the path of the future.

Of course, this essay deserves an A. It is well organized, full of pertinent and efficiently incorporated evidence, and answers the question directly, insightfully, and fully. Essentially, both students used the same evidence, but the second writer handles it better. This is partly because the question itself lends itself well to an organized response. The "significance" question leaves the field too wide open for most students, and we cannot fault them for not intuiting that we wanted a more sophisticated answer. If we truly want to assess our students' thinking process, we have to set them up for success, give them adequate time to develop theories about the content, and give them feedback that helps them understand where they were successful and where they were not.

Assessing discussions and written responses are quite different. In the assessment of a discussion, we step in very occasionally to shape the nature of (but not the content of) their discourse as the discussion is happening, as well as spending other class periods deliberately explaining the metacognitive aspects of inference, reasoning, implications, and so on.

For written responses, the burden is on us to design questions that elicit the level of sophistication we want, and we can also show them examples of a well-organized paragraph, an insight well expressed, and the efficient and effective use of evidence. As we focus more on the development of critical thinking skills, we ourselves will become more aware of how it works, while at the same time bringing this crucial skill into the foreground so that students, too, become familiar with it. We can refine our methods as we go.

Here are some improved essay questions:

Not: What are some of the hardships caused by environmental damage?

But: In your opinion, what are the three most important steps the US can take to reduce environmental damage?

Not: How does the tone/diction/figurative language and the like contribute to the text?

But: How does the tone/diction/figurative language change the dynamic of the text?

Not: Describe the process of photosynthesis/cell division/respiration/absorption.

But: Create a detailed, annotated diagram that explains the contribution that the process of photosynthesis/cell division/respiration/absorption makes to the body.

Not: Why does character x act as he/she does?

But: What cultural norms of the times does this character adhere to and which does the character reject, and why?

Not: What are the strengths and weaknesses of idea/proposal/interpretation x?

But: Which of the ideas/proposals/interpretations has the most merit and the least disadvantages, and why?

Now you can practice some critical thinking of your own. What is the common denominator in the improved questions? Take some time to develop a theory before reading further.

The common denominator is that the improved questions cause the student to consider the context of the question, which should lead to a more organized and insightful response, as long as the student has done plenty of critical thinking on the topic.

Let's consider another scenario. Two teachers are using online discussion boards when they decide (after some cajoling by administrators) to turn their class into a "blended" class, which means cutting out two face-to-face class periods a week. With less time to develop ideas, will the quality of class discussions suffer? Or, with some changes to the way the discussion boards are used, can their meaningfulness increase so that time spent in class goes straight to the good stuff?

Why not try? The teachers kick some ideas around and then realize that if they design discussion board as the students' workspace, not just a place to prove they read, they might get more out of it. So instead of asking questions like, "Why does character *x* commit act *y*?," they put students into different topic groups and ask each group to develop a theory about what the author was up to.

They do not grade students' performance online but instead privately contact students who seemed not to be putting in enough effort or thought. Other than that, they stay out of their students' way, not seeding their ideas and intervening only very occasionally. For example, if the students in one group start going in circles, the teacher posts the message: "You're going in circles. Can someone break the logjam?" The teachers assess their students' thinking by what they say online, noticing inferences, implications, comparisons, pattern recognition, and so on, using this valuable information as feedback on the effectiveness of the assignment instead.

The teachers resist the very strong temptation to prod students when they drop a fruitful idea, and they fight back the urge to articulate their ideas better for them. To do so simply trains students to wait until the teacher weighs in; then they follow the teacher's line of thinking instead of coming up with their own. This robs them of their opportunity to practice critical thinking, a skill we teachers already have and don't need to demonstrate to them. Instead, we need to focus our critical thinking on how we set up our assignments and assess them.

The students note the sea change, or metamorphosis, in the class philosophy—the fact that this homework is not busy work but is designed for their benefit. Because they are charged with thinking about theory, they quickly push through clarifying details like plot and character elements in order to get to the critical thinking process of developing a theory, which they enjoy. In fact, these kinds of conversations occasionally take place between some of the students—often the night before their essays were due—as they help each other succeed in the class. Now their conversations can be out in the open and legitimate, not secretive.

As a result of their work online, in-class discussions become more efficient and productive, such that missing two class meetings per week is not a problem. In fact, the teachers each allocate one of those periods as time for students to come and work together in their rooms, where they can consult with them about their ideas if they want. Discussion boards become more collegial and important.

To shift to assessing thinking, the following are some potential categories to assess along with suggested traits to analyze the various activities the students perform, including direct dialogue with individual students. The list is not meant to be comprehensive—it's just a starter kit. Each teacher will want to create a unique list to fit the kind of critical thinking they want their students to practice in a given course.

What to Look For

Improved thinking as evidenced by more:

- Insightful observations
- Identifying patterns and anomalies
- Eagerness to ponder competing theories
- Engagement with students whose ideas differ
- Ability to build on other students' ideas
- Ability to synthesize opposing views
- Willingness to take intellectual risks
- Sophistication in verbal, written, and visual expression

Growing independence and self-direction as evidenced by:

- Fewer questions for teacher
- Fewer attempts to hide behind the work of others
- More openness to ambiguity
- Less neediness in and out of class
- More confident expression of ideas
- More curiosity about and enthusiasm for the topic and course

Better schemas and analogies as evidenced by:

- A shift from seeking correct answers to seeking understanding
- More efficient retrieval of concepts with related ideas and information
- Ability to apply concepts to other data
- Ability to make fruitful connections and comparisons
- Ability to explain concepts through analogy, metaphor, or logic
- Independent use of the concepts in discourse and problem solving
- Increasing skill and independence in knowing how to learn in this discipline

Mastery of threshold concepts as evidenced by:

- An ability to explain the threshold concept and its implications
- A tendency to approach new problems with better strategies
- Expressing the concept as a known and familiar truth
- A stronger sense of purpose in and identification with the discipline
- Being self-directed and self-correcting in deploying concepts

Note that these traits may not necessarily occur in a particular sequence. Students have different capacities and resistances and will find their own path to competence and mastery if given the right environment to practice thinking in the discipline. But overall, students should move from seeking "the" answer and adequate proof to seeking to construct knowledge.

Once the students' critical thinking has been assessed, we can advise each of them about how to improve. The student who produces a lot of information but little organization can work on creating categories for her knowledge. She might need to create an idea map to decide which categories can be broken down into others and to decide how to represent the relationships between ideas. The student who presents a good "bottom-line" summary needs to learn how to back up his claim with pertinent evidence and logical reasoning. He can practice this by taking a couple of his summary statements and explaining them in writing. Both students should also try to explain the metacognitive process they go through so that they begin to understand the process of critical thinking.

Students who consistently get things wrong need to probe their own ideas before they present them. They can work on a list of questions to ask themselves: Is this idea central? Is it important? Are there at least three pieces of evidence I can use to support my claim? Do I need to go back and study my information again? If the student can create a generic list of questions for self-probing—and use them—she will have come a long way in teaching herself how to think more productively.

The student who, rather than offer his own ideas, offers criticism of others' ideas is practicing a good skill but may need to work on tact, as well as to be encouraged to make original comments and possibly to work on synthesizing opposing ideas. Having learned how to synthesize opposing ideas might soften his approach to criticizing others because he will have found some value in each idea.

Synthesizing ideas is difficult and takes time, so students who can do this may not contribute until rather late in the discussion. If they have been thinking, the time was not wasted! Working with students on their particular weaknesses in critical thinking can be fascinating. The mind is amazing—a combination of brilliant insights, stubborn habits, sticky misperceptions, biases, empathy, endless capacity to learn, and limitless imagination. What other job can be more rewarding that improving young minds?

The traits we want to measure may not be perceivable by traditional assignments, quizzes, and tests. Shifting to assessing critical thinking in the discipline requires some creativity in designing assessment tools and opportunities to focus on how students express their thinking. It might also entail changes in the way discourse is practiced in the classroom to allow more opportunities for listening to students' logic and for asking questions.

For further reading, see Appendix G, "How to Assess Critical Thinking."

Such a major change in assessment procedures leads to the question of grades. Does it still make sense to give an overall grade for a given assignment? Or would grading by specific thinking skills make more sense? A more targeted kind of grading would reinforce the importance of thinking like a practitioner because it would isolate specific skills instead of assigning a global grade per assignment. For example, an English literature essay could be graded on multiple categories:

- Vividness of language
- Boldness and ideas
- Development of ideas
- Clarity of organization
- Mechanical accuracy

Yes, that's five grades versus one, but it gives the student a better picture of overall performance, and there's no need to grade each assignment on all categories. In addition, rather than write lengthy comments, codes can be assigned to each category. One could simply write, for example, *Viv+* in the margin of an essay where the language is vivid, *Dev-* in a paragraph where the ideas are not well developed, and so on, as in figure 6.2.

In this form of grading, both student and teacher can see the work's strengths and weaknesses at a glance. Then assigning a grade for each category would just entail noting how many pluses there are versus minuses, upgrading or downgrading scores depending on the quality of the thought or choice of evidence. The grade book now portrays the student's progress in each category over time. Conferences can focus on specific skills, and students can decide for themselves which category to work on first.

Meanwhile, in class, the teacher offers lessons in each category—for example, having students zoom in on "What, if anything, is wrong/right with" samples of mediocre and successful expressions and having them revise weaker statements to make then more vivid, better developed, and so on. Again, asking students to think deeply and to discern the difference between mediocre and successful attempts will eventually lead to their mastering the concepts in the categories and carrying these skills forward as they continue their education.

Different categories or criteria can be developed for specific courses. In a history course, for example, the discussions, essays, and projects could be graded on thesis, evidence, and argument, with codes *T-* for a poor thesis, *E+* for good evidence, and *A-* for inadequate argument. Assignments in environmental science could be scored on things like evidence, breadth of environmental impact analysis, and feasibility of proposed solutions. It can actually take less time to score assignments in this way, while conveying more pertinent and focused feedback to students.

Teacher-Annotated Student Essay

Even though the three-day Battle of Antietam was a draw, it was a significant event in the Civil War. In one day of September 1862, more than 22,000 soldiers died, making it the <u>bloodiest day</u> in American military history. General Robert E. Lee, after a few successful battles with the Union Army, <u>marched boldly</u> into Maryland, Union territory, in order to <u>threaten Washington DC</u>. But a union soldier found a copy of his field orders (wrapped around three cigars) and notified Union General George McClellan, who had been sitting tight, fearing (incorrectly) that he was outnumbered. His army actually outnumbered Lee's by two-to-one. With the information about Lee's plans, McClellan, who was <u>notorious</u> for delaying too long before entering a battle, <u>uncharacteristically</u> took the initiative and for a time pushed back the Confederate forces. However, he failed to press for a decisive victory, allowing Lee to regroup and to set up his artillery. Then he failed to send orders to his troops, and each commander had to decide what to do on his own; one unit never joined the battle at all. Eventually both sides lost so many men that the two generals agreed to a truce. Lee retreated. Both generals were criticized by the press for their performance. The battle is significant in that no land was gained or lost on either side, though the human cost was deplorable. In addition, the fact that Lee retreated back to the South improved President Lincoln's status in the eyes of the populace and led him to issue the Emancipation Proclamation.

Idea-

Viv

]
] **Viv**
]
] **Dev+**
]
] **Viv**
] **Dev**
]

] **Dev-**
] **Org-**

Idea+

Mech+

Viv	**B+**
Idea	**B-**
Dev	**B**
Org	**C**
Mech	**A**

Figure 6.2.

Conclusion

Implementing the major conceptual changes described in this book will require thought, planning, and innovation. A teacher might want to tackle one lesson, one unit, or one idea at a time and assess the process and results. Pushing the responsibility for thinking onto the students changes the teacher's role considerably and actually places more demands on the teacher's content knowledge, both in choosing clear, unambiguous source materials that raise interesting questions and in answering students' impromptu questions.

Giving over control to the students to learn places demands on the teacher to know enough to be able to field the wide array of potential questions that come up in the course of discussion, requiring teachers to know the map of all the seas in their discipline, not just one sea-lane. This can be downright frightening. But there's nothing wrong with saying, "Let's look it up." As we experiment with modeling instruction, asking students to develop analogies, choosing clear, focused source materials, we might not get the process fully right the first time, but with time and experience, it will become more comfortable, efficient, and enjoyable. The results can be profoundly significant, and success is addictive.

It's important to recall that teachers, too, grapple with several threshold concepts when they redesign their classes and may have to overcome some resistance, some flux in understanding, and some lapses in true mastery before feeling confident. Teachers become learners who must objectively measure which parts of the process are working and which are not, just as we hope our students will (re)learn to do. It's humbling to experience what our students feel as they encounter new concepts, but it gives us insights into how thinking works, into how to do our jobs more effectively.

Appendix A

How People Learn

In this appendix, and in appendices B, C, D, and G, are additional quotations from some of the sources consulted during the research for this book. Hopefully, some of them will inspire you to read further on a given topic and clarify what you have already read. There is plenty of research about how people learn best, and now we teachers can take advantage of this knowledge.

In their 2011 book *Making Thinking Visible: How to Promote Engagement, Understanding, and Independence for All Learners*, Harvard education consultants Ron Ritchhardt, Mark Church, and Karin Morrison explain how traditional teaching often fails to develop critical thinking skills: "In most school settings, educators have focused more on the completion of work and assignments than on a true development of understanding. Although this work can, if designed well, help to foster understanding, more often than not its focus is on the replication of skills and knowledge, some new and some old" (34).

In their 2000 book *How People Learn: Bridging Research and Practice*, editors M. Suzanne Donovan, John D. Bransford, and James W. Pellegrino summarize research by the National Research Council showing three key findings. All three are relevant to this book.

1. "Students come to the classroom with preconceptions about how the world works. If their initial understanding is not engaged, they may fail to grasp the new concepts and information that are taught, or they may learn them for purposes of a test but revert to their preconceptions outside the classroom." (10)
2. "To develop competence in an area of inquiry, students must: (a) have a deep foundation of factual knowledge, (b) understand facts and ideas in the context

of a conceptual framework, and (c) organize knowledge in ways that facilitate retrieval and application." (12)

3. "A 'metacognitive' approach to instruction can help students learn to take control of their own learning by defining learning goals and monitoring their progress in achieving them." (13)

They further explain that

> Knowledge of a large set of disconnected facts is not sufficient. To develop competence in an area of inquiry, students must have opportunities to learn with understanding. Deep understanding of subject matter transforms factual information into usable knowledge. A pronounced difference between experts and novices is that experts' command of concepts shapes their understanding of new information: it allows them to see patterns, relationships, or discrepancies that are not apparent to novices. They do not necessarily have better overall memories than other people. But their conceptual understanding allows them to extract a level of meaning from information that is not apparent to novices, and this helps them select and remember relevant information. Experts are also able to fluently access relevant knowledge because their understanding of subject matter allows them to quickly identify what is relevant. Hence, their attention is not overtaxed by complex events. (12)

Professor of psychology Joan Lucariello along with David Naff (2009) in their American Psychological Association web article "How Do I Get My Students over Their Alternative Conceptions (Misconceptions) for Learning?" explain why students resist new (threshold) concepts that contradict their current misconceptions.

> It is important for teachers to know about the preconceptions of their students because learning depends on and is related to student prior knowledge. . . . We interpret incoming information in terms of our current knowledge and cognitive organizations. Learners try to link new information to what they already know. . . . This kind of learning is known as assimilation. . . . When new information is inconsistent with what learners already know it cannot be assimilated. Rather, the learner's knowledge will have to change or be altered because of this new information and experience. This kind of learning is known as accommodation (of knowledge/mental structures). . . . Alternative conceptions (misconceptions) interfere with learning for several reasons. Students use these erroneous understandings to interpret new experiences, thereby interfering with correctly grasping the new experiences.

If students resist new learning, teachers must develop lessons that compel them to face their misconceptions and grapple with information. This means designing lessons that cause these encounters, as in the challenge problems described above.

In his 2008 book *Visible Learning: A Synthesis of over 800 Analyses Relating to Achievement*, education professor John Hattie asserts that despite the hundreds of teaching methods available, the most effective methods cause students to create knowledge themselves. This represents a total sea change in how we approach our teaching—to focus not on *what* students know but on *how well they think* in the discipline, how far they are advancing as practitioners. In his conclusion, he explains what it will take for teachers to achieve this:

> It is about the power of passionate, accomplished teachers who focus on students' cognitive engagement with the content of what it is they are teaching. It is about teachers who focus their skills in developing a way of thinking, reasoning, and emphasizing problem-solving and strategies in their teaching about the content they wish their students to learn. It is about teachers enabling students to do more than what teachers do unto them; it is the focus on imparting new knowledge and understanding and then considering and monitoring how students gain fluency and appreciation in this new knowledge and build conceptions of this knowing and understanding. It is how teachers and students strategize, think about, play with, and build conceptions about worthwhile knowledge and understanding. Monitoring, assessing, and evaluating the progress in this task is what then leads to the power of feedback—which comes second in the learning equation. Feedback to students involves providing information and understanding about the tasks that make the difference in light of what the *student* already understands, misunderstands, and constructs. Feedback from students to teachers involves information and understanding about the tasks that make the difference in light of what the *teacher* already understands, misunderstands, and constructs about the learning of his or her students. (237–38)

Further, "Teachers need to move from the single idea to multiple ideas, and to relate and then extend these ideas such that learners construct and reconstruct knowledge and ideas. It is not the knowledge or ideas, but the learner's construction of this knowledge and these ideas that is critical" (239). Why multiple ideas? Because to oversimplify the threshold concept can lead students to process it only partially, or to memorize a simplified version of the concept. When the concept has not been fully explored and compared to the student's own perceptions, it probably will not get integrated with what she already knows, and thus may not be convincing enough for the student to alter her misperceptions.

In his 2010 book *Why Don't Students Like School? A Cognitive Scientist Answers Questions about How the Mind Works and What It Means for the Classroom*, Daniel T. Willingham explains how thinking works and how to design class problems that are neither too difficult nor too easy, so that our students' curiosity gets engaged and they learn how to think. Here are a few insightful passages:

> People are naturally curious, but we are not naturally good thinkers; unless the cognitive conditions are right, we will avoid thinking. (2)

> The sorts of mental work that people seek out or avoid also provide one answer to why more students don't like school. Working on problems that are of the right level of difficulty is rewarding, but working on problems that are too easy or too difficult is unpleasant. Students can't opt out of these problems the way adults often can. (13)

> From a cognitive perspective, an important factor is whether or not a student consistently experiences the pleasurable rush of solving a problem. What can teachers do to ensure that each student gets that pleasure? Be Sure That There Are Problems to Be Solved. By

problem I don't necessarily mean a question addressed to the class by the teacher, or a mathematical puzzle. I mean cognitive work that poses moderate challenge, including such activities as understanding a poem or thinking of novel uses for recyclable materials. This sort of cognitive work is of course the main stuff of teaching—we want our students to think. But without some attention, a lesson plan can become a long string of teacher explanations, with little opportunity for students to solve problems. So scan each lesson plan with an eye toward the cognitive work that students will be doing. How often does such work occur? Is it intermixed with cognitive breaks? When you have identified the challenges, consider whether they are open to negative outcomes such as students failing to understand what they are to do, or students being unlikely to solve the problem, or students simply trying to guess what you would like them to say or do. (19)

Jan H. F. Meyer and Ray Land in their 2006 *Overcoming Barriers to Student Understanding: Threshold Concepts and Troublesome Knowledge* recognize students' resistance to knowledge that challenges their worldview, making it important that teachers reassure students that struggles are normal when the learning is deep and important: "Another strategy is for teachers frequently to reassure students in what-ever ways they can (informally, assignment feedback, etc.) that not knowing, or glimpsing and then losing, is part of coming to know" (201).

University physics professor David Hestenes (1979) in his article "Wherefore a Science of Teaching?" explains how Piaget's stages of cognitive development, which culminate in "an increasingly complex system of reasoning patterns or schemes" (6), help explain why students need to develop schemas themselves. By "concrete thinkers," Piaget means students who have not yet developed operable schemas in a discipline and who are generally less aware of their own thinking and discovery pro-cess than are more cognitively developed students. Hestenes also finds it reprehen-sible that traditional physics courses cater to students who have already developed advanced reasoning skills rather than create opportunities for all students to become adept at physics reasoning and critical thinking:

> It is commonly believed that proportional reasoning is taught in high school algebra courses when students are introduced to the formula $a/b = c/d$. On the contrary, Piaget's theory implies that a student cannot comprehend the formula unless he is already ca-pable of proportional reasoning. (7)

> Empirical studies show that the majority of American high school students reason at the Concrete level. How do such students cope with high school algebra? Since they do not possess the conceptual structures [schemas] needed to fully understand algebraic symbol-ism, they must resort to alternative strategies such as rote memorization. It is to be ex-pected, then, that their abilities to recall and handle algebraic relations will decline rapidly after they have completed the course. The relation of cognitive level to long-term retention of algebra has not been systematically studied, but science teachers continually encounter students who seem to remember nothing at all from their high school algebra courses. It is hard to escape the conclusion that conventional high school algebra courses are a total waste of time for Concrete thinkers. This is not to say that Concrete thinkers cannot learn algebra, but only that they need instruction to help them develop formal operations. (7)

In his 2013 book *Assessing Historical Thinking and Understanding: Innovative Designs for New Standards*, history professor Bruce A. VanSledright draws attention to the wide disconnect between what we now know about learning and the way, at least in history classes, we continue to teach. "Our common teaching-learning-testing strategies are rooted in outdated assumptions about how children and adolescents learn" (105). "It would be fair to say that how we typically test in history misses the mark rather profoundly" (8). He then describes what students need to demonstrate to verify that they have mastered skills of historical thinking: "Students will need to be able to 'cite,' 'support' (analysis), and 'connect' (insights). In the second case, they must be able to 'evaluate,' 'determine,' and 'acknowledge.' The third case requires 'evaluation' again, along with 'corroborating' and 'challenging.' These verbs represent thinking capabilities by any other name" (10). When a student can articulate a threshold concept clearly, and can use the terminology of the idea with apparent ease and accuracy, the teacher can detect that the student has or is mastering the concept. It's a matter of careful listening to what the student says, careful reading of what the student writes. When the ideas get expressed in a rote or inaccurate manner, the student has not yet crossed the threshold into having a corrected worldview regarding the material and needs to continue to explore the information relating to it. He also needs to try to defend the misconceptions he holds, until at last he modifies his view and accepts a more fitting interpretation of how the world works. The teacher cannot simply tell the student the threshold concept. The student has to create the concept in his own mind and store the supporting information along with it.

Appendix B

Analogy as the Core of Cognition

The concept of analogy as central to understanding and learning is a huge revelation from cognitive science. Reading about it is fascinating and will lead to noting how routinely we employ metaphors and analogies when we speak, especially when we try to explain something. Tapping into this mechanism of understanding has the potential to revolutionize teaching.

In his 2007 book *The Stuff of Thought: Language as a Window into Human Nature*, cognitive scientist, linguist, and Harvard professor of psychology Steven Pinker explores our use of language and concludes that analogy and metaphor are central to all human thinking.

> I think that metaphor really is a key to explaining thought and language. The human mind comes equipped with an ability to penetrate the cladding of sensory appearance and discern the abstract construction underneath—not always on demand, and not infallibly, but often enough and insightfully enough to shape the human condition. Our powers of analogy allow us to apply ancient neural structures to newfound subject matter, to discover hidden laws and systems in nature, and not least, to amplify the expressive power of language itself. (176)

Douglas Hofstadter (2006), a renowned cognitive scientist who has spent most of his professional life studying the role of analogy in thinking, explains in "Analogy as the Core of Cognition" that analogy is the way we think, from childhood on, and that analogies are useful because they organize information into useful schemas that can be quickly applied to new problems, almost intuitively.

> One should not think of analogy-making as a special variety of reasoning (as in the dull and uninspiring phrase "analogical reasoning and problem-solving," a long-standing

cliché in the cognitive science world), for that is to do analogy a terrible disservice. After all, reasoning and problem-solving have (at least I dearly hope!) been at long last recognized as lying far indeed from the core of human thought. If analogy were merely a special variety of something that in itself lies way out on the peripheries, then it would be but an itty-bitty blip in the broad blue sky of cognition. To me, however, analogy is anything but a bitty blip—rather, it's the very blue that fills the whole sky of cognition—analogy is everything, or very nearly so, in my view.

[I offer a] shift [in viewpoint] to suggest that every concept we have is essentially nothing but a tightly packaged bundle of analogies, and to suggest that all we do when we think is to move fluidly from concept to concept—in other words, to leap from one analogy bundle to another—and to suggest, lastly, that such concept-to-concept leaps are themselves made via analogical connection, to boot.

In their journal article "Modeling Instruction: An Effective Model for Science Education," college physics instructors Jane Jackson, Larry Dukerich, and David Hestenes (2008) concur that analogies and metaphors are central to thinking, and that teachers should design their courses, using modeling instruction, around helping students "straighten out their metaphors":

In Modeling, instead of designing the course to address specific "naive conceptions," the instructor focuses on helping students construct appropriate models to account for the phenomenon they study. When students learn to correctly identify a physical system, represent it diagrammatically, and then apply it to the situation they are studying, their misconceptions tend to fall away. (13)

George Lakoff and Mark Johnson in their seminal 1980 book *Metaphors We Live By* also assert that metaphor is central to thinking:

Metaphors are not merely things to be seen beyond. In fact, one can see beyond them only by using other metaphors. It is as though the ability to comprehend experience through metaphor were a sense, like seeing or touching or hearing, with metaphors providing the only ways to perceive and experience much of the world. Metaphor is as much a part of our functioning as our sense of touch, and as precious. (239)

Appendix C

Student Retention with Schemas and Analogies

In this appendix, you'll find the results of studies of retention rates using modeling instruction. Modeling instruction is just one (very good) method to challenge students to confront their misconceptions and revise their mental schemas. Professors of physics who promote and use modeling instruction have performed substantial and impressive studies to verify that having students grapple with problems before learning formulas and develop their own theories is superior to other teaching methods.

In the 2000 final report of a six-year study of Modeling Instruction for the National Science Foundation, "Findings of the Modeling Workshop Project (1994–00)," lead investigator David Hestenes outlines results demonstrating that modeling instruction almost doubles student retention compared with that of traditional physics instruction:

- The average FCI pretest score for students beginning high school physics is about 26%, slightly above the random guessing level of 20%, with few scores over 30%.
- The average FCI posttest score after traditional (teacher-centered) instruction is 42%. Therefore, at least 2/3 of the students failed to reach a minimal [60%] understanding of physics in their high school course. . . .
- After teachers have completed the first 4-week Modeling Workshop (novice modelers), their students have an average FCI posttest score of 53%—clear evidence for improved instruction.
- More than a third of the teachers who have completed the full two-summer program of Modeling Workshops can be described as expert modelers, meaning that they have adopted and fully implemented the Modeling Method of Instruction with evident understanding. For 647 students of 11 expert modelers, the average FCI posttest score was 69%, and several of these experts consistently

have average student scores close to 80%. These are among the very best results reported for high school and even college physics. (1)

> From our observations, the most important factor in student learning by the Modeling Method (partly measured by FCI scores) is the teacher's *skill in managing classroom discourse*. That, of course, depends on the teacher's own ability to articulate the models clearly and explicitly as well as use them to describe, explain, predict and control physical processes. (2)

Physics professors Jane Jackson, Larry Dukerich, and David Hestenes (2008), in "Modeling Instruction: An Effective Model for Science Education," report that when Professor Frances Lawrenz, an independent external evaluator for the National Science Foundation, evaluated their modeling instruction program, he said:

> I have almost never seen such overwhelming and consistent support for a teaching approach. It is especially surprising within the physics community, which is known for its critical analysis and slow acceptance of innovation. In short, the modeling approach presented by the project is sound and deserves to be spread nationally. (16)

In his article "Modeling Methodology for Physics Teachers," Hestenes (1996) explains why students cannot understand what we say when our information clashes with their internal schemas.

> Unaware that their own ideas about force differ drastically from those of the teacher, most students systematically misunderstand most of what they read and hear in traditional introductory physics. Consequently, they cannot understand why they fail at problem solving and they are forced to resort to rote methods for learning meaningless formulas and procedures. The result is frustration, humiliation, and student turnoff! (4)

And also in "Modeling Instruction: An Effective Model for Science Education" (Jackson, Dukerich, and Hestenes 2008), the authors repeat this idea, saying that "Since students systematically misunderstand most of what we tell them (due to the fact that what they hear is filtered through their existing mental structures), the emphasis is placed on student articulation of the concepts" (13).

In other words, we cannot know if students have adequately processed information and built reliable analogies in their minds without assessing how they explain and use the concepts.

Appendix D

Threshold Concepts and Skills

Professor of psychology Joan Lucariello, along with David Naff (2009) in their article "How Do I Get My Students over Their Alternative Conceptions (Misconceptions) for Learning?" list how and how not to lead students to face their misconceptions. They suggest the following:

> Use model-based reasoning [such as "thought experiments" and "hypothetical scenarios"], which helps students construct new representations that vary from their intuitive theories. . . . Present students with experiences [challenges] that cause cognitive conflict in students' minds. Experiences . . . that can cause cognitive conflict are ones that get students to consider their erroneous (misconception) knowledge side-by-side with, or at the same time as, the correct concept or theory. . . . Once students have overcome their alternative conceptions (misconceptions), engage them in argument to strengthen their newly acquired correct knowledge.

They also suggest that source materials be "anomalous" yet "credible," not "ambiguous," but varied. And they add that teachers should "engag[e] students in justification of their reasoning," because "if students engage in a process called 'self-explanation,' then conceptual change is more likely."

Jan H. F. Meyer and Ray Land, who first introduced the theory of threshold concepts in 2003, define them in their 2006 *Overcoming Barriers to Student Understanding: Threshold Concepts and Troublesome Knowledge*:

> A threshold concept is conceived in a quite different way [from other course learning]. From the point of view of the expert, it is an idea which gives shape and structure to the subject, but it is inaccessible to the novice. In fact, it may be counter-intuitive in nature and off-putting. It can appear to be a denial of the world which the student experiences and it may therefore lead to the student rejecting the subject as "abstract" and "meaningless." (75)

They also explain why threshold concepts are so difficult to teach:

> There are two sources of trouble here for the teacher. First, if a threshold concept is introduced too early it is inaccessible to the student and it can only be learnt in a rote fashion which emphasizes its lack of real meaning to the student. Second, once a student has acquired sufficient knowledge and understanding to make it possible for the concept to play an integrative role, the teacher has to help students to re-interpret their current ideas in the light of the threshold concept. This is a major undertaking and, if it fails, the student fails to truly "get inside" the subject. In either case the teacher and the student may settle for the appearance of understanding which is all that can be achieved if the threshold concept is not acquired. (76)

And why they should not be simplified by the instructor:

> There appear to be important implications for the manner in which students are initially introduced to threshold concepts. It is speculated that in the acquisition of threshold concepts "first impressions matter." Efforts to make threshold concepts "easier" by simplifying their initial expression and application may, in fact, set students onto a path of acquiring the concept as a form of "ritualized" (routine and meaningless) knowledge that actually forms a barrier to the acquisition of the concept in a transformative sense. This conclusion impacts on what might otherwise be advocated as good pedagogic practice; namely, an introductory simplification of transformative concepts that some students experience difficulty in acquiring. (100)

And they explain how threshold concepts are transformational, irreversible, integrative, bounded, and troublesome for learners.

> The transformative character of threshold concepts reflects the way in which they can change an individual's perception of themselves as well as their perception of a subject. In gaining access to a new way of seeing, an individual has access to being part of a community. The irreversibility of a threshold concept makes it inconceivable that they would return to viewing not only the world around them, but also a subject community and themselves, in the way they did before. The integrative quality of a threshold concept is critical to these first two characteristics. When an individual acquires a threshold concept the ideas and procedures of a subject make sense to them when before they seemed alien. It is the threshold concept that provides coherence. Fourth, a threshold concept necessarily helps to define the boundaries of a subject area because it clarifies the scope of a subject community. Finally, a threshold concept is very likely to be troublesome because it not only operates at a deep integrating way in a subject, but it is also taken for granted by practitioners in a subject and therefore rarely made explicit. (74)

Here Meyer and Land explain how students in the process of learning a threshold concept feel as though they are in a liminal or uncertain place:

> [Students sense of kind of] liminality . . . a suspended state in which understanding can approximate to a kind of mimicry or lack of authenticity. Also an unsettling—a sense of loss. You have to let go of previous ideas. One oscillates from feeling like one gets it,

then loses that feeling. We want them to stay in that fluid state of liminality so that their ideas won't become crystalized. You [student and teacher] have to envision a version of yourself doing/being the new you with that skill, and at first it seems like you are doing it from a script. Subjectivity is discursive, part of the construction of a self that is never really fixed. (139)

On their website Decoding the Disciplines, Arlene Diaz, Joan Middendorf, David Pace, and Leah Shopkow (2014) identify three bottlenecks to learning and seven steps for identifying course threshold concepts.

Three types of bottlenecks to learning may be unearthed: 1) procedural obstacles in which students have not mastered the steps that are necessary for successfully completing the tasks required in a course; 2) epistemological bottlenecks in which students fail to understand the basic nature of knowledge construction in a discipline; and 3) emotional bottlenecks in which students' affective reaction to the nature of the discipline or of the subject matter hinders learning. In all cases the purpose of Decoding is to set in motion a series of steps (modeling, practice and feedback, motivation, and assessment) that will allow larger numbers of students to enter the learning process.

The seven steps are as follow:

1. Identify bottlenecks. Where in a course are significant numbers of students having difficulty mastering basic material?
2. Define the processes that students need to master to get past the bottlenecks. What would experts in the field or advanced students do to get past the bottleneck?
3. Model these processes. How can these steps be made clearly visible to students?
4. Create opportunities to practice these processes and to get feedback on them. How can each of the steps identified be captured in specific assignments or exercises?
5. Motivate students to move through these processes. What emotional obstacles interfere with this learning and how can they be minimized?
6. Assess student mastery of these processes. How can we know the extent to which these interventions have been successful?
7. Share what has been learned. What has been discovered in this process and how can this be most effectively shared with others?

Pace and Middendorf (2004) explain each step in "Decoding the Disciplines: Helping Students Learn Disciplinary Ways of Thinking."

Appendix E

Sample Threshold Concepts and Skills

Below are representative threshold concepts and skills from a variety of disciplines. These lists are not meant to be prescriptive for all courses of their kind but rather samples to help teachers develop their own course's threshold concepts—the larger truths that experts intuitively understand and that students find difficult or even counterintuitive.

THRESHOLD CONCEPTS IN AP ENGLISH LITERATURE

- Texts are designed both in content and style to expose a societal/human flaw or strength.
- The reader actively constructs meaning in interpreting a text.
- Poems hold competing ideas in eternal conflict.
- Essays open up, rather than shut down, further thought (i.e., essays should not be predictable and dull).
- Critical theory provides an intellectual lens that offers new, competing interpretations of a text.
- Art brings to the foreground the ideas that are in flux in the society so that they can be interrogated instead of simply accepted as part of the setting.

SKILLS IN AP ENGLISH LITERATURE

- Student can identify and explain the contribution of literary devices (metaphor, understatement, allusion, etc.) and strategies (irony, point of view, etc.).

- Student actively engages in class discussions and makes pertinent, meaningful comments.
- Student challenges and defends ideas with tact, grace, and integrity.
- Student collaborates openly and effectively with peers to explore ideas, forge arguments, debate evidence, and generate new insights.
- Student writes of significant ideas with insight, clarity, style, pertinent evidence, and logical analysis.

THRESHOLD CONCEPTS IN HISTORY (GRADES 9 AND 10)

- History is marked by cyclical patterns, repeated over time and place.
- Change over time is not linear, predetermined, or progressive.
- Each historian creates a new historical interpretation, inflected by her own values and education and those of the culture that nurtured her.
- The compound causes of historical events are multiple and varied, as well as often being hidden and elusive.
- There is often a mismatch between intent and outcome that complicates the meaning and morality of historical decisions.
- Societies (and individuals) define themselves in opposition to an "other."
- Countervailing forces rarely achieve equilibrium (e.g., revolutions spawn counterrevolutions).
- There is a historical tension between the distribution and consolidation of resources and power.
- Beliefs can overwhelm and distort facts.
- Our access to the past is limited to the material artifacts and residual ideas that remain in our current culture.

SKILLS IN HISTORY

- Student uses pertinent evidence and explains its significance.
- Student takes initiative in using data provided by a variety of media (e.g., primary and secondary texts as well as statistical data and artifacts).
- Student realizes the incomplete nature of the historical record and pays attention to what is and is not in the data.
- Student takes into account the varying perspectives of those involved and directly affected by the event as well as the perspectives of later interpreters.
- Student is able to create explanatory theses.
- Student understands historical complexity.
- Student develops empathy for people of different places and times.
- Student identifies patterns, forces, and contextual influences.

THRESHOLD CONCEPTS IN ENVIRONMENTAL SCIENCE

- The role of uncertainty in environmental science makes it difficult to convey the importance of attending to ongoing environmental damage.
- There is a tragic disconnect between who benefits from and who pays for the environmental damage in our world.
- Species extinction alters food chains and diminishes forever the richness of nutrition and the potential for natural medicines.
- Our planet's resources are finite and need to be managed carefully and responsibly, not left to market demands.
- Although we cannot always see it, the world is interconnected in a way that makes us all vulnerable to environmental damage, no matter where we are.
- The way that we oversimplify our calculation of renewable and nonrenewable energy production masks serious, ongoing environmental damage.
- Agricultural land used for either meat or grain production incurs costs such soil erosion, depletion, and pollution that are not represented in cost analyses.
- We cannot achieve sustainable growth until businesses, governments, and individuals adopt the "triple bottom line" approach to production and consumption costs by considering the social, environmental, and economic impacts (or "people, planet, and profits") of what we do.
- Market prices, including those of consumer goods, carbon credits, and alternative energy sources, do not reflect externalities.
- The collective actions of individuals have the potential to create both environmental problems and solutions.
- Many human endeavors have unintended consequences on the environment, even measures taken to protect it.
- Every individual action has a net consequence on the environment.
- Third world countries have a better chance of meeting greenhouse gas emission goals than developed nations because they have no existing infrastructure and therefore can design infrastructure that supports alternative energy sources.

SKILLS IN ENVIRONMENTAL SCIENCE

- Student takes ownership of the process of observation, explanation, and hypothesis creation.
- Student uses reliable evidence to make a point.
- Student seeks to determine bias in sources.

THRESHOLD CONCEPTS IN BIOLOGY

- A testable hypothesis must be feasible but also allow for counterexamples.
- In bioenergetics (photosynthesis and respiration), energy is not created or lost, just transformed.

- Cell surface-area-to-volume ratios impact cell efficiency.
- Water movement (diffusion and osmosis) continues when equilibrium is reached, but there is no net gain or loss in volume.
- Cell membranes are selectively permeable, with varying pathways depending on the complexity of the substances involved.
- Genetics (protein synthesis, cell division, DNA) is the basis of growth and reproduction. Random changes (mutations) can lead to adaptive advantages in heritable traits over generations.

SKILLS IN BIOLOGY

- Student can interpret and produce accurate graphs, diagrams, and data, can fully explain them, and fully understands the concept of scale.
- Student actively assesses probability during experimentation and analysis.
- Student takes ownership of the process of observation, explanation, and hypothesis creation.
- Student uses biological terms correctly and spontaneously.
- Student understands and enjoys the investigative nature of biology.

THRESHOLD CONCEPTS IN ECONOMICS

- Opportunity cost, or the cost of forgoing a different choice, is the real cost of any decision and must be factored into decision making.
- The law of comparative advantage suggests that countries that produce goods at a lower opportunity cost should specialize in what they produce most efficiently and trade for other goods with the countries best at making those other products.
- The existence of scarcity, the idea that resources are limited but consumer demands are unlimited, requires people to make choices.
- Economic thinking requires that one engage in marginal analysis (the additional costs and benefits of any choice) and consider those additional costs and benefits in order to make the best decision.
- Externalities, the costs borne by third parties and not the producer or consumer, should be factored into total costs.
- Macroeconomic indicators (trade deficits, employment rates, inflation, currency, interest rates, government debt and deficit) are neither inherently negative or positive: they must be analyzed in context.
- Since humans can never learn all the facts of a production or consumer choice, they are often limited by their "bounded rationality," the information that they know. They should make allowances for unknown factors and search further when feasible.
- Because of the complexity of market forces and the impracticality of conducting controlled experiments, economists often must analyze scenarios with only

partial data along with the assumption of *ceteris paribus*, that all else remains the same.

- Because of the circular flow of money and resources, markets for products and resources are interdependent.
- Markets are efficient at maximizing the use of society's resources in most cases. However, there are situations where markets fail to achieve these benefits due to spillover costs and benefits, imperfect information, and the distortion of competition by the existence of large, powerful firms.
- At some time in the production process, the additional use of resources will reach a point of diminishing returns.
- Increases and decreases of the supply of money affect price levels and economic productivity.
- Anything that serves as a medium of exchange, a store of value, or a unit of account effectively is money.

SKILLS IN ECONOMICS

- Student exhibits the ability to prepare and decode data and graphs and fully understands what they explain.
- Student exhibits facility in choosing which concepts to apply to a given problem.
- Student takes ownership of the process of analysis, explanation, and hypothesis creation.
- Student uses economic terms accurately and spontaneously.
- Student understands and enjoys the intricate nature of economics.

THRESHOLD CONCEPTS IN PHYSICS

Note: In the physics subfield of mechanics, physics education research frames the issue of threshold concepts in terms of preconceived notions, the ideas about force and motion that people almost universally develop to explain the world as they explore and grow up. Mechanics is a minefield of such preconceived notions, but a few stand out as particularly troublesome keystone concepts around which the others constellate. The concepts below are numbered to indicate the order of teaching them.

1. Acceleration is discriminated from velocity not only in that it involves speeding up but also because the velocity's magnitude or direction changes in one unit of time: Most students start their study of physics with indistinct concepts in which velocity and acceleration are relatively equivalent descriptors of motion, but then progress to the idea that acceleration means speeding up, and then move to the more mathematically precise idea that acceleration is how much the object speeds up in one unit of time. After that point, the concept must

be enlarged to include slowing down, then refined to the change in velocity in one unit of time in order to include changes in direction.

2. Balanced forces result in constant velocity motion (including a constant of velocity of zero), while unbalanced forces cause acceleration: Although many students can glibly state Newton's First Law in the form "An object in motion stays in motion, an object at rest stays at rest, unless it experiences an outside force," when asked to apply this concept they universally fall back on impetus, explaining that an object will not move unless it experiences an unbalanced force or that more force is required to have a faster, constant velocity. Since force causes acceleration, and not velocity, a person whose motion concept does not discriminate between velocity and acceleration has no chance to figure out what the force is actually causing.

3. Force is an interaction between two objects; "passive" objects like a table or the floor also exert forces; force is always action: We develop our metaphor of force based on forces that we apply by pushing or pulling on other objects, but this often misleads students to conclude that "passive" objects like a table or the floor cannot exert forces. It helps to develop a microscopic picture of these objects as made of atoms and how those atoms interact at the surface boundary between two objects.

4. When one object (A) exerts a force on another object (B), B exerts an equal and opposite force on A: Once again, students can usually recite a glib version of Newton's Third Law, "For every action there is an equal and opposite reaction," before entering their physics class. But nevertheless they still believe that the larger, more powerful, or more active element will exert the greatest force, or that the object that was most affected by an interaction received the most force.

5. If an object is already moving, a force applied at right angles to the direction of motion will cause it to accelerate by changing directions, not by speeding up or slowing down. A force applied at some other angle can cause speeding up or slowing down and a change of direction at the same time. After passing through the prior thresholds or at least getting stuck in the liminal state, students still tend to believe that unbalanced forces must cause speeding up or slowing down.

SKILLS IN PHYSICS

- Student can interpret and produce accurate graphs, diagrams, and data and can fully explain them.
- Student makes and records careful observations.
- Student actively questions assumptions.
- Student takes ownership of the process of setting up experiments, observation, explanation, and hypothesis creation.
- Student uses reliable evidence to make a point.
- Student uses physics terms accurately and spontaneously.
- Student actively undertakes and enjoys the investigative nature of physics.

Appendix F

Sample Student Challenges

ENGLISH LITERATURE CHALLENGE

Threshold concepts for this challenge:

1. Texts represent ideas current in the society and times in which they are produced and serve to bring important topics to the attention of the public.
2. Art brings to the fore the ideas that are in flux in the society so that they can be interrogated instead of simply accepted as part of the setting.

Challenge: Read Don DeLillo's novel *White Noise*. In groups of three, find evidence in the novel of social trends or ideas specific to the time and society in which DeLillo set it. Which trends or ideas are accepted as given and which are interrogated in the novel? Draw a diagram on a whiteboard that shows the relationships between ideas that are accepted and those that are interrogated. Develop a theory of why the novel came out when it did, with the ideas that it has. What is the role of art in society? Write down your theory as a clear, sentence-long thesis that expresses a central truth about what you discovered. If you uncovered more than one truth, write a separate sentence for each. Be prepared to explain your theory using a diagram. The group must reach consensus, and each member must be equally capable of explaining your group's ideas.

HISTORY CHALLENGE

Threshold concepts for this challenge:

1. The compound causes of historical events are multiple and varied, as well as often being hidden and elusive.
2. There is a historical tension between the distribution and consolidation of resources and power.
3. History is marked by cyclical patterns repeated over time and place.

Challenge: How did the transcontinental railroad in the United States affect the economy, society, politics, and ideas? (In some classes, the teacher could assign a different topic to each group; in others, all the groups could analyze the same topic.) The groups should diagram the dynamics caused by the railroad and brainstorm several areas of change, progress, or deterioration. Then develop a theory that explains your changes. Next, consider how network technologies such as the telegraph and cell phones affect the economy, society, politics, and ideas. Develop a theory for why the changes occur. Is the theory for networks similar or different from your railroad theory? Why or why not? Write down your theory as a clear, sentence-long thesis that expresses a central truth about what you discovered. If you uncovered more than one truth, write a separate sentence for each. Be prepared to explain your theory using your diagram. All members of the group must be equally capable of explaining your group's ideas.

ENVIRONMENTAL SCIENCE CHALLENGE

Threshold concepts for this challenge:

1. Many human endeavors have unintended consequences on the environment, even measures taken to protect it.
2. Every individual action has a net consequence on the environment.
3. Species extinction alters food chains and diminishes forever the richness of nutrition and the potential for natural medicines.
4. Although we cannot always see it, the world is interconnected in a way that makes us all vulnerable to environmental damage, no matter where we are.
5. There is a tragic disconnect between who benefits from and who pays for the environmental damage in our world.

Note: In environmental science, we analyze all topics through the triple bottom line, considering the social, environmental, and economic impacts of what we do.

Challenge: Watch the documentary *America's Lost Landscape: The Tallgrass Prairie* about the destruction of the tallgrass prairie biome, commonly referred to as the

Great Plains. (The cinematography is beautiful, and plenty of archival photos bring to life the period between 1830 and 1900, when the tall prairie grasses were transformed into wheat fields and then into nutrient-impoverished dust, though new ecological preservation efforts may restore some of the Great Plains' former beauty and productivity.)

List some good and bad outcomes you noted in the film, considering such things as whether the land was used properly or improperly, how the farmers and cattle ranchers played into the transformation, as well as how the local Native Americans were affected, whether the tribes farmed or hunted.

Analyze your selected topics with the triple-bottom-line method: identifying the effects on economic, social, and environmental factors. In your groups of three, draw a triangle on a whiteboard and label the triangle corners with triple-bottom-line factors. Next overlay a diagram of some of your good and bad effects, indicating which of the three factors (economic, social, environmental) was involved, and indicating the most dominant effects by size or color. Show any overlaps as well. Write down your theory as a clear, sentence-long thesis that expresses a central truth about what you discovered. If you uncovered more than one truth, write a separate sentence for each. Be prepared to explain your theories using your diagram. All members of the group must be equally capable of explaining your group's ideas.

BIOLOGY CHALLENGE

Threshold concepts for this challenge:

1. The cellular metabolic process of respiration is a combustion reaction that produces energy.
2. The permeability of cell membranes accounts for the diffusion and homeostasis necessary for processing food into energy.

Challenge: How do cells use energy and matter? You will start with the processes of larger organisms and work your way down to the cell level. Examine food chains to confirm that every organism needs a food source and can be a food source. What is food, and what are the organic macromolecules in food? What happens during digestion? Trace the acquisition, transfer, storage, and elimination of the matter and energy in four different complex organisms. Compare the energy acquisition in a fungi-yeast organism to a plant's acquisition of food. What differences did you note? Create a whiteboard that traces the movement of energy through each level of each of the organisms. You will have several systems to diagram, so decide how best to portray them. Do the more complex organisms acquire, transfer, store, and eliminate energy differently from simple organisms? Explain why what happened did happen. Write down your theory as a clear, sentence-long thesis that expresses a central truth about what you discovered. If you uncovered more than one truth, write a separate sentence for each. Members of the group must achieve consensus and must be equally capable of explaining your group's theory and reasoning.

ECONOMICS CHALLENGE

Threshold concepts for this challenge:

1. Opportunity cost, or the cost of forgoing a different choice, is the real cost of any decision and must be factored into decision making.
2. Economic thinking requires that one engage in marginal analysis (the additional cost and benefits of any choice) and consider those additional costs and benefits in order to make the best decision.
3. Markets are efficient at maximizing the use of society's resources in most cases. However, there are situations where markets fail to achieve these benefits due to spillover costs and benefits, imperfect information, and the distortion of competition by the existence of large, powerful firms.

Challenge: Your task is to decide whether health-care costs follow the typical supply–demand curve such that making choices in treatment options can be analyzed effectively by considering opportunity costs and margin analysis. First, read and discuss the sources within your group and draw a diagram on your whiteboard representing the entities involved in health care in the United States. Use arrows to indicate flows of money, and use the relative size of objects to indicate more or less influence on outcomes. Don't forget to include the uninsured health-care patient as well. Who makes decisions in health-care treatment? How do these decisions affect the well-being of people in the United States? What marginal-analysis factors must be considered, and which entities act on this analysis? What problems appear, and how can they be dealt with? Develop a theory about the way health care works in the United States. Write down your theory as a clear, sentence-long thesis that expresses a central truth about what you discovered. If you uncovered more than one truth, write a separate sentence for each. Be prepared to explain your theory using your diagram. All members of the group must reach consensus and be equally capable of explaining your group's ideas.

PHYSICS CHALLENGE

Threshold concepts for this challenge:

1. Acceleration is discriminated from velocity not only in that it involves speeding up but also because the velocity's magnitude or direction changes in one unit of time.

2. Balanced forces result in constant velocity motion (including a constant of velocity of zero), while unbalanced forces cause acceleration.

Challenge: Your teacher has drawn a circle with a four-foot diameter on the floor. Push a bowling ball around the circle with a broom. You will push the bowling ball around the edge of the circle as fast as you can, while keeping the ball on the circle. Before starting, come up with a working hypothesis of what will happen. When you are ready to try the experiment, have someone tape the event from above (stand on a chair or use a selfie stick and iPhone). While one person is pushing the bowling ball, the others are encouraging her to move quickly and observing the mechanics of what happens. Next, stop pushing the ball with the broom. What happens and why? As a group, draw a diagram of what happened, showing the circle, the direction the ball goes, the direction of each broom push, and the direction the ball went when no longer being pushed. Agree on the diagram, then revisit your hypothesis and write a new one, if necessary. Explain why what happened did happen. Write down your theory as a clear, sentence-long thesis that expresses a central truth about what you discovered. If you uncovered more than one truth, write a separate sentence for each. All members of the group must reach consensus and must be equally capable of explaining your group's theory and reasoning.

Appendix G

How to Assess Critical Thinking

Perhaps the shift to assessing thinking rather than knowledge will be the most challenging piece of adopting the ideas in this book. It's a big shift, requiring a different way of paying attention to the students and a different way of thinking about teaching and learning. Here are some additional thoughts on how to accomplish this goal.

Jan H. F. Meyer and Ray Land in their 2006 *Overcoming Barriers to Student Understanding: Threshold Concepts and Troublesome Knowledge* insist that the assessment of students' thinking process should begin before the concept is taught, with listening:

> Teaching for understanding of threshold concepts needs to be preceded by listening for understanding. In terms of what we will refer to below as "pre-liminal variation" in the ways in which students approach, or come to terms with, a threshold concept, we can't second guess where students are coming from or what their uncertainties are. It is difficult for teachers, experienced and expert within the discipline, who have long since traveled similar ground in their own disciplinary excursions, to gaze backwards across thresholds and understand the conceptual difficulty or obstacles that a student is currently experiencing. . . . Learning to understand what the students do not understand requires "cultivating a third ear that listens not for what a student knows (discrete packages of knowledge) but for the terms that shape a student's knowledge, her not knowing, her forgetting, her circles of stuck places and resistances" (Ellsworth, 1997: 71). The acquisition of a "third ear" might also discourage teachers from making hasty judgments about students' abilities and foster appreciation of the tough conceptual and emotional journeys they have to make. (199–200)

In their article "How Do My Students Think: Diagnosing Student Thinking" professor of psychology Joan Lucariello and David Naff list strategies that teachers can employ to assess how well students are thinking in a course. Teachers should do the following:

1. Conduct quizzes (pretests).
2. Try to learn how students are going about solving problems or arriving at their answers. Knowing the ideas and/or strategies that students are using to arrive at an answer (whether the answer is right or wrong) can be very informative for the purposes of making instructions more effective.
3. Encourage your students to ask questions and then examine the content of those questions.
4. Ask students to define major concepts, then analyze their definitions for errors in logic or strategy (the rule) that are causing the students to make mistakes.
5. Use the technique of "differential diagnosis" [list possible explanations, rule out unusual ones, consider common reasons].
6. Use the technique of DFA (Difficulty Factors Assessment [figure out where the tough spots are]) to identify which features of a problem are either causing student difficulty or facilitating student learning.
7. Present problems to students in which you systematically vary important features of the problem.
8. Provide common misconceptions among the answer choices on a quiz (i.e., multiple choice) or in response to classroom questions.
9. Give "implicit-confidence" tests. These tests involve a simple modification of the traditional multiple-choice test.
10. Administer questionnaires in specific subject matter areas in order to identify whether a misconception is unique to a particular context or is due to a problem with general reasoning or language.
11. Administer a categorization/sorting task.
12. Have students model (draw or use props) their solutions to a problem and analyze their models for pattern or strategy errors.
13. Use student memory/recall of problems and definitions as a window into their thinking.

Teachers should do the following:

1. Do not jump too quickly to one hypothesis about student thinking processes or reasoning. Prematurely focusing on one hypothesis about what a student may be thinking can cause you to be unaware of competing hypotheses that may provide a better explanation.
2. Do not stick with or lock onto only one type of response behavior a student may display. Vary problem features to determine whether the same response behavior is displayed under different problem conditions.

3. Do not make a diagnosis about students' logic, reasoning, or thinking processes on the basis of their performance on one problem or one kind of problem.

4. When probing students' understanding, try to avoid asking only general, open-ended questions. And don't stop probing after asking one question. Follow-up questions can reveal the source of a misconception, or an error in reasoning or strategy selection. Follow-up questions are also important when a student gives the right answer. Remember that faulty thinking can occasionally lead to correct answers.

The guidelines provided in chapter 6 will also prove helpful. Learning to assess critical thinking skills may take some time, but it's extremely revealing of how well we are actually teaching our students. If we can shift our own point of view from teaching content to that of teaching thinking, the students will benefit greatly, and will probably enjoy the course more than ever. So will we.

Recommended Reading and Viewing

American Modeling Teachers Association. http://modelinginstruction.org.

Atherton, John. 2010. "Introducing Threshold Concepts 1." Vimeo. https://vimeo.com/11583202.

Coven, Robert, and Carole Hamilton. 2009. "Modeling Instruction in the Humanities." SlideShare.

Donovan, Suzanne, John D. Bransford, and James W. Pellegrino, eds. 1999. *How People Learn: Bridging Research and Practice*. Washington, DC: National Academy Press. http://www.nap.edu/catalog/9457/how-people-learn-bridging- research-and-practice.

Hattie, John. 2008. *Visible Learning: A Synthesis of over 800 Analyses Relating to Achievement*. London: Routledge.

Hattie, John, and Gregory C. R. Yates. 2013. *Visible Learning and the Science of How We Learn*. London: Routledge.

Hofstadter, Douglas. 2006. "Analogy as the Core of Cognition." Presidential Lecture at Stanford University, February 6. YouTube.com. https://www.youtube.com/watch?v=n8m7lFQ3njk.

Lakoff, George, and Mark Johnson. 1980. *Metaphors We Live By*. Chicago: University of Chicago Press.

Land, Ray. 2010. "Threshold Concepts and Troublesome Knowledge: A Transformative Approach to Learning." Keynote Address at the New Zealand Association of Bridging Educators Ninth National Conference. https://teaching.unsw.edu.au/threshold-concepts-and-troublesome-knowledge-transformative-approach-learning. (See especially slides 15–23 and 47–56.)

Meyer, Jan H. F., and Ray Land, eds. 2006. *Overcoming Barriers to Student Understanding: Threshold Concepts and Troublesome Knowledge*. London: Routledge.

Willingham, Daniel T. 2009. *Why Don't Students Like School? A Cognitive Scientist Answers Questions about How the Mind Works and What It Means for the Classroom*. San Francisco: Jossey-Bass.

References

Bransford, John D., Ann L. Brown, and Rodney R. Cocking, eds. 2000. *How People Learn: Brain, Mind, Experience, and School.* Washington, DC: National Academies Press.

Diaz, Arlene, Joan Middendorf, David Pace, and Leah Shopkow. 2014. "Decoding the Disciplines." http://decodingthedisciplines.org/.

Donovan, M. Suzanne, John D. Bransford, and James W. Pellegrino, eds. 2000. *How People Learn: Bridging Research and Practice.* Washington, DC: National Academies Press.

Gardner, Howard. 2006. *Multiple Intelligences: New Horizons in Theory and Practice.* New York: Basic Books.

Hattie, John. 2008. *Visible Learning: A Synthesis of over 800 Analyses Relating to Achievement.* London: Routledge.

Hattie, John, and Gregory C. R. Yates. 2013. *Visible Learning and the Science of How We Learn.* London: Routledge.

Hestenes, David. 1979. "Wherefore a Science of Teaching?" *Physics Teacher* 17 (4): 235–42.

———. 1996. "Modeling Methodology for Physics Teachers." *Proceedings of the International Conference on Undergraduate Physics.* http://modeling.asu.edu/R&E/ModelingMeth-jul98.pdf.

———. 2000. "Findings of the Modeling Workshop Project (1994–00)." http://modeling.asu.edu/R&E/ModelingWorkshopFindings.pdf.

Hestenes, David, and Jane Jackson. 2008. "Physics Workshop for School Technology Infusion." http://modeling.asu.edu/R&E/ModelingMeth-jul98.pdf.

Hestenes, David, Malcolm Wells, and Gregg Swackhamer. 1992. "Force Concept Inventory." *Physics Teacher* 30:141–66.2. doi.org/10.1119/1.2343497.

Hofstadter, Douglas. 2001. "Epilogue: Analogy as the Core of Cognition." In *The Analogical Mind: Perspectives from Cognitive Science*, ed. Dedre Gentner, Keith J. Holyoak, and Boicho N. Kokinov, 499–538. Boston: MIT Press.

———. 2006. "Analogy as the Core of Cognition." Presidential Lecture at Stanford University, February 6. YouTube.com. https://www.youtube.com/watch?v=n8m7lFQ3njk.

Jackson, Jane, Larry Dukerich, and David Hestenes. 2008. "Modeling Instruction: An Effective Model for Science Education." *Science Educator* 17 (1): 10–17.

Lakoff, George, and Mark Johnson. 1980. *Metaphors We Live By.* 2nd ed. Chicago: University of Chicago Press.

Lucariello, Joan, and David Naff. 2009. "How Do I Get My Students over Their Alternative Conceptions (Misconceptions) for Learning?" American Psychological Association. http://www.apa.org/education/k12/misconceptions.aspx.

———. 2013. "How Do My Students Think: Diagnosing Student Thinking" American Psychological Association. http://www.apa.org/education/k12/student-thinking.aspx.

Marzano, Robert, Debra Pickering, and Jan Pollock. 2001. *Classroom Instruction That Works: Research-Based Strategies for Increasing Student Achievement.* Alexandria, VA: Association for Supervision and Curriculum Development.

Meyer, Jan H. F., and Ray Land. 2006. *Overcoming Barriers to Student Understanding: Threshold Concepts and Troublesome Knowledge.* London: Routledge.

Meyer, Jan H. F., Ray Land, and Caroline Baillie, eds. 2010. *Threshold Concepts and Transformational Learning.* Rotterdam: Sense.

Pace, David, and Joan Middendorf. 2004. *Decoding the Disciplines: Helping Students Learn Disciplinary Ways of Thinking.* New Directions for Teaching and Learning 98. San Francisco: Jossey-Bass.

Piaget, Jean. 1955. *The Construction of Reality in the Child.* Translated by Margaret Cook. London: Routledge and Kegan Paul.

Pinker, Steven. 2007. *The Stuff of Thought: Language as a Window into Human Nature.* New York: Penguin.

Ritchhardt, Ron, Mark Church, and Karin Morrison. 2011. *Making Thinking Visible: How to Promote Engagement, Understanding, and Independence for All Learners.* San Francisco: Jossey-Bass.

Time. 1999. "The Great Minds of the Century." March 29.

VanSledright, Bruce A. 2013. *Assessing Historical Thinking and Understanding: Innovative Designs for New Standards.* New York: Routledge.

Willingham, Daniel T. 2010. *Why Don't Students Like School? A Cognitive Scientist Answers Questions about How the Mind Works and What It Means for the Classroom.* San Francisco: Jossey-Bass.

Index

accommodation, 70
accountability: in modeling instructions, 46; of students, 29, 46
adverbs, 47
analogies, *xiv*, 27, *39*; assessment of, 62; brain and, 9; categorization and, 9–10; cognition and, xvii, 9, 10, 75–76; first, 7; memory and, 8; problem-solving and, 75–76; retention and, 77–78; schemas and, 5–6, 9; tactile, 7; theory development and, 29; understanding and, 39; visual, 6–8. *See also* metaphors
anecdotes, 11
Assessing Historical Thinking and Understanding: Innovative Designs for New Standards (VanSledright), 73
assessment, 14, 17, 32, 40; of analogies, 62; changing, 53; in class discussion, 55–57, 60, 61; design, 63; DFA, 96; English examples of, 64; through essays, 57–64, 65; methods, 95–97; of schemas, 62; theory development and, 60; of thinking process, 60–63, 95; threshold concepts and, 21, 62, 95; tools, 63; traditional, 73; in written responses, 57–64, 65

beliefs, 11, 23; challenging, 20; facts and, 29. *See also* worldview

bias, 39
bioenergetics, 23
biology: challenge, 91–92; skills in, 86; threshold concepts in, 85–86
book selection, 36
brain: analogies and, 9; hippocampus, 46–47; information and, xiii, 6; language and, 47; learning process and, xv; learning styles and, xiv; memory and, 46; of students, 7
Bransford, John D., 69–70

capitalism, 22
categorization, 5; analogies and, 9–10; intelligence and, 9. *See also* schemas
challenges, 89–93
children: development of, 1; knowledge acquisition of, 11; learning of, 1–2, 9, 33; misconceptions of, 1–2; thinking of, 2; understanding of, 25; worldview of, 2
Church, Mark, 69
circular reasoning, 11
citizenship, of students, xv
class discussions: assessment in, 55–57, 60, 61; discussion boards and, 61; example of, 56–57; interruptions of, 56; listening during, 57; teachers and, 61
classroom dynamics, xiii